Frank & Kathy,

AUTISM
TRANSLATED

5 Keys to Help You Understand & Connect
With Teens and Adults on the Spectrum

*You were there at the birth of
this book! It has changed a bit
since then. Thank you so much for
your feedback & support.*

by Toni Boucher

Much respect,

Toni Boucher

A Genius Book

Published by
Genius Publishing
Mount Pleasant, SC 29464

Cover Photo "antonia150" by Gerardo Leccese
Cover Design by Toni Boucher
Edited by Aaron V and Helen Wells

Printed and bound in the United States of America
First Edition

Title ID: 6290821
ISBN-13: 978-1533376947

Dedicated to
those of you who refused to jaywalk in kindergarten, played hooky from recess
in junior high and now drive the speed limit
&
André comme moi mais libre de forger une nouvelle voie

With Gratitude. . .

To my parents who didn't let me walk across the highway to Dairy Queen on my own in first grade but never once said a goal is too big or far away to reach. My daughter Diana, Sue Taylor, Mick Prangsbøll, Jodi Cholewicki, Ken Spidle, Myra Brouwer, Steven Paglierani, Dennis Brouwer and Anthony Alexander provided candid feedback when I needed it. Anthony Alexander, Steven Paglierani and Jodi Cholewicki also listened patiently as I talked through ideas that needed to be developed. My editors Aaron V and Helen Wells combed diligently through the manuscript and gave me the push I needed to complete this project. Aaron V and Mick Prangsbøll also made sure that the narrative and case studies accurately represented the autistic experience from their points of view. Dr. Laura Carpenter provided feedback and guidance on "The Autism Screening Tool for Women". She along with Bob Egelson, Dr. Lucia Horowitz and Susan Clark each shared their expertise through the years in ways that influenced the shape of this book. Thanks to Hector Salazar and Dan Gosselin of MeanStream Studios for marketing and distribution. Mary Bauer who should really be the subject of a book unto herself gave me the opportunity to work on the manuscript during our time together. Gerardo Leccese who creates beautiful art with everything he touches graciously allowed for the use of the headshot for the front cover. And finally, to all of those individuals who have shared their stories and experiences and helped to develop autism friendly screening tools with the intention of making life a little easier for future generations of the autism family, I offer my utmost respect, appreciation and love.

TABLE OF CONTENTS

How to Use This Book

This book has stories, narrative explanations, case studies and exercises for you to complete and is intended to be a flexible "how to". You can choose to read from beginning to end working through the exercises as you go or read through once and complete the exercises at a later time. There is a checklist at the end of each chapter for you to keep track of the exercises you have completed.

While each of the five keys build on each other, each chapter can stand alone. So if you have a particular question or area of concern that you would like to read about first such as; what is autism? (pg 9), problem behaviors (pg 49), sensory challenges (pg 63), communication (pg 99), or socialization and connection (pg 131), then by all means, jump ahead to the relevant chapter.

A note on Terminology

Most people who have a diagnosis or have self-identified prefer to be called "autistic" instead of "person with autism". Therefore, the term "autistic" is used in the narrative throughout <u>Autism Translated</u> except for those cases where someone is directly quoted.

THE RESET BUTTON

*A*t 18 months I took no notice of my mother's absence at the park when she hid behind a tree. My mother chalked this up to an independent free spirit but couldn't quite say the same about my painting obsession with black spots which had her wondering if she had unwittingly done something to psychologically "damage" me. To her immense relief I did eventually outgrow the black spots and traded them in for "rainbows, flowers and budderfies" two years after the black spot painting spree began.

But I was still inconsolable and "came unglued" over seemingly insignificant events like the car moving before my seatbelt was completely fastened and the sensation from tags and seams which made getting dressed a painful morning ritual for everyone involved. Ironically I went barefoot whenever I had the chance, even in the snow.

I was the kid who snuck into an empty classroom to play hooky from recess, completely mystified even frightened by children my own age who engaged in what I perceived as unpredictable and illogical behaviors.

I spent a lot of time spinning around in circles and watched people's mouths when they talked to me so I could avoid looking into their eyes.

I spoke "like a little adult" with expansive vocabulary and complex sentence structure that amused my parents and confused my peers. When I was 8, the other girls got together and told me I was stuck up because of the way I talked. Their comment punctuated the awkwardness that I felt but had not risen yet to my conscious recognition. From that point on I made a deliberate effort to censor every word and do my best to talk like the other kids.

At age 13 the other teens in my neighborhood were having sprinkler parties. I was reading Shakespeare, Chaucer and the dictionary. But not just any dictionary. It had to be The English Oxford Dictionary. I was relieved to have books as an excuse to turn down invitations to these puzzling social gatherings where kids would deliberately spray each other with water. And while I avoided the unpredictability of a water fight, behind closed doors I would stare at the faucet mesmerized by the liquid flowing between my fingers.

I studied every ethnic costume known to the western world in detail and could correctly identify their origin in a line up. I had absolutely no idea why other girls my age wanted autographs from Michael Jackson or Prince. It was not "logical" to want the signature of someone you didn't even know.

At school I missed more days than I attended. The doctor could find no reason for my chronic "sickness" and because I made good grades, followed the rules and got along well with adults no one except my mother worried much or noticed that anything was amiss.

To this day, I get overwhelmed when ordering from the menu at Starbucks or making a purchase with cash, refuse to enter Walmart during Christmas season, read every single word on the cereal box, follow elaborate rituals in public restrooms, require several days of isolation to recover from a rare appearance at a party and forget to ask for help when I am lost on the road. If I am completely honest, I still occasionally get sidetracked watching water pour from the faucet.

While I have managed to fly mostly under the radar with my quirky behaviors, my daughter Diana flew straight into it. She had punched enough holes in walls, melted down enough in the grocery store and struggled enough in school to draw the attention of psychologists by the time she was 6. At 11 she received an autism spectrum diagnosis and underwent speech therapy for central auditory processing.

Close colleagues and friends tease me about my quirky habits and call me an "undiagnosed aspie". They say Diana didn't get all of her qualities from her dad and that my career choice and life-long attraction to people on the spectrum is the result of an underlying familiarity and shared common experience.

Perhaps they are right. What I do know for certain is this: My own sensitivities, ritualistic behaviors and difficulties with relationships caused me to question the methods of autism treatment and the attitude towards people on the spectrum that were prevalent in the field when I started years ago. I ignored much of what I was taught. Instead I made it a point to listen to as many autistic people as I possibly could. I wanted to understand their points of view. I wanted to know what worked for them.

I found their observations and advice to be very accurate and effective in getting positive outcomes. And through the years, common themes began to appear in spite of the many different personalities and life experiences that each of these individuals had. The core message that ultimately emerged in each of these cases is simple yet profound: Forging a healthy understanding and connection is critical to ensure autistic people can live happy, well-adjusted lives.

On the flip side, ignorance, prejudice and refusal to understand the autism spectrum can and often do result in serious consequences.

I have worked with individuals who were: falsely convicted of crimes they did not commit, unknowingly caught in bankruptcy, traumatically committed to psychiatric hospitals, chemically restrained (heavily med-icated to control behaviors), homeless, estranged from families, fired from jobs, kicked out of school, financially or sexually exploited, and addicted to alcohol or other drugs (often opiates).

In most of these instances, these problems could have been avoided simply with the right knowledge, understanding and a little support. These are the worst case scenarios, but even in the best of circumstances, when people have tremendous resources and fulfilling lives, this does not diminish the hard work and unending determination to overcome adversity that has contributed to their successes.

This book was written specifically about the unique circumstances faced by teens and adults whose concerns and challenges may slip through the cracks or go unrecognized and unsupported because autism does not always show up in the ways that people expect. It is not always obvious. As children grow up they develop coping skills, gain under-standing and learn new ways to function. As a result, autism becomes less noticeable. But it is still there.

Many of the children I have worked with started out with "classic" signs of autism (non-verbal, spinning in circles, no eye contact, flat facial expressions and grew up to develop wonderful language and skills to relate with others but may still struggle or need support in some capacity. This book is certainly applicable to them as much as it is to the aspie adult who never got a diagnosis and holds things together without any outside help. If you care about a teen or adult who:

✓ might have autism/Asperger's

✓ has a formal diagnosis of autism/Asperger's

✓ is self identified

✓ or possesses some noticeable autistic traits

and you would like to better understand and connect with them, then this book was written just for you.

Although there is significant research and literature to assist families of young autistic children in this process of awareness and under-standing, there is limited information available to help teens and adults through the specific challenges and concerns that we face whether we are dealing with issues like eviction, starting a conversation, going off to college or asking someone out on a date.

This guide is designed to fill that gap by serving as a bridge between the non-autistic world and the autistic world. My role is merely to be a "translator" to help make that bridge as smooth and understandable as possible so that you can cross over successfully.

Notice that I made no reference to people on the autism spectrum crossing this bridge to meet you. That is because autistic people are already constantly doing this every day in ways you might never imagine- in therapy, a walk past the perfume counter at the mall or even when we simply leave the bedroom.

When you step over this bridge and meet us on our terms in our world, you connect with us on a level that goes beyond words and actions, beyond therapy sessions, interventions and training manuals. You connect where the spirit or essence of our common humanness resides in spite of our outward differences. This is where real *soul*utions" to problems reside. The term "*soul*ution" is no mistake. "Solutions" prevent outward behaviors like hand flapping, pacing or body rocking.

"*Soul*utions" create the environment and conditions for people to feel safe, accepted and honored for who they are without any need to pretend to be someone they are not. "*Soul*utions" make room for people's inherent but oftentimes hidden abilities, strengths and unique qualities to shine forth.

This book is not about how the experts define autism or the therapies they recommend. It is written from the point of view of hundreds of individuals who have worked through life experiences and developed their own understanding of what it means to be autistic both as individuals on the spectrum and as supportive family members.

While each of us is unique there are several themes that repeatedly emerge in spite of our differences. The following chapters break these common themes down into 5 key areas where a change in your thinking can lead to meaningful improvements for someone on the spectrum and your ability to relate to them.

Understanding & Connection

Key #5
Relate to Me

Key #1
Redefine Autism

Key #4
Learn My Language

Key #2
Turn "Problems"
Into Strengths

Key #3
Understand How
Sensory Integration
& Anxiety Affect
My Life

The Goal

Whether you read each page and complete every exercise or skim through to find the case studies, your role while reading this book is simply to evaluate the assumptions that you have held about people on the autism spectrum and replace any of those ideas that have not been helpful with more useful ways of thinking. In other words, we are asking you to push the reset button on your ideas about autism. That's it! If you can do that after reading this book then we will have been successful.

If you care about someone on the spectrum and have felt the frustration and heartache of not knowing how to connect or support them adequately through the challenges they face, this book will help you do that. Jim Sinclair writes of this process in his poignant essay, "Don't Mourn for Us":

> *The ways we relate are different. Push for the things your expectations tell you are normal, and you'll find frustration, disappointment, resentment, maybe even rage and hatred. Approach respectfully, without preconceptions, and with openness to learning new things, and you'll find a world you could never have imagined.*

You have been invited on a journey to enter this world and you have the cumulative voices of hundreds of individuals and their families to guide you. We want to help you understand what it is like for someone on the spectrum to exist in a largely non-autistic world. All you need to do is keep reading with an open mind and listen to what we have to say.

No I am not like Rain Man.
Mick Prangsbøll

Autism is unseen.
Sue Taylor

Key # 1
Redefine Autism

Martha was a slender, leathery woman in her fifties who wore a continually jaded expression on her face and spoke about whatever came to her mind without putting it through a filter. She had no known family or friends and you could set your clock by the sound of her car leaving for her job at a local assembly plant each morning.

I had been assigned to assist Martha through a non-profit organization designated to support individuals with autism because she had been kicked out of her apartment for "repeatedly picking fights" with the other tenants and needed help to find a new place to live.

At first Martha appeared on all accounts to be "typical" as far as I could tell. She was able to talk about her job, kept her place clean and her car well maintained. Perhaps she just needed some anger management classes to address her temper. But as I spent time with this woman, telltale signs of something curious and unusual began to unfold.

There was the $50 baby gift she purchased on a fixed income for a family she hardly knew at work. Then one day, I arrived late and when I explained that I had been in a little fender bender, Martha's reply was "OK. We should get started now."

Another day we showed up for a 1:30 appointment with someone named June to look at a potential apartment and when the receptionist asked Martha to fill out some paperwork and informed us that we could meet with her when it was complete, Martha bristled and replied "But it is 1:30 and I have an appointment with June at 1:30!"

"Yes." Replied the receptionist with a smile on her face. "Just fill out this paperwork and June will be right with you."

"But it is 1:30 and I have an appointment with June at 1:30!" The receptionist's smile faded.

"I understand, but you need to fill this paperwork out first."

Martha stated it louder this time. "But it is 1:30 and I have an appointment with June at 1:30!" She seemed oblivious to the attention she was drawing to herself or the fact that it wasn't imperative to meet at *exactly* 1:30.

Martha was giving me my first on the job training in adult autism and I was beginning to understand how she had been kicked out of her apartment not because she had anger management issues, but because she was extremely literal and straightforward in a world that was neither literal or straightforward, and it was creating a tremendous amount of confusion and anxiety for her.

"I don't mean to be rude." She explained the incident that led to her eviction. "The guy was walking his dog in the courtyard and he's not supposed to do that. I just told him he couldn't have his dog in there. Then he said he could do whatever he damn well pleased and I told him that is not true. Neighborhood covenants strictly forbid it."

As I spent more time with Martha, I began to clearly see the areas where she needed assistance and support in addition to her unique talents and gifts. She wasn't callous towards others as I had assumed by her response to my fender bender- she just didn't know how to process and converse about an unexpected event like a car accident so she just didn't talk about it at all.

As a matter of fact, Martha came to demonstrate a tremendous depth of compassion as she meticulously cared for every wayward dog and fretted over her coworkers whenever they came down with the slightest cold.

I admired her honesty and the fact that she was unaffected by issues like social status and the inevitability of death.

Our challenge in getting Martha the right supports was that people had a hard time acknowledging that she even needed assistance in the first place.

Martha decided to approach the landlord at her existing apartment to see if he would understand her situation and agree to let her remain if she developed some new skills to deal with her neighbors more effectively. "You can't have autism. You work and you drive. There is nothing wrong with you." He was adamant and uncompromising. But even more than that, he seemed angry towards Martha for even suggesting that she was autistic.

Agency workers said the same thing when we requested assistance. And Martha would comment to me, "I need help. The problem is that I LOOK normal, but I'm NOT normal. If I was carrying around an oxygen tank or limped, something you could see, then people would help me. "

Martha is not alone. Since autism can present in many subtle ways and can remain unrecognized, those of us who struggle are often mis-understood, misdiagnosed and mistreated, our issues remaining largely unaddressed. And because we don't always fit the "classic" or stereo-typical notion of what autism is we may not even realize that our own repeated difficulties in education, work and relationships are a result of having autistic characteristics until we reach our 30's, 40's, 50's or even later, if at all.

Instead we may just recognize that the normal day-to-day activities of life and relationships tend to cause us more trouble and require more effort to manage than they do for other people.

Common Myths about Autism

The general stereotype is that there are two kinds of people on the spectrum: those who are "smart" or "high functioning" and those who are "not".

Autism Really Is a Spectrum

A spectrum is a scale with two "extreme ends". People on the autism spectrum can be anywhere on this scale, not just either end. Mary for example may have extreme sensory and social challenges, while Brian may have mild sensory challenges and extreme social communication barriers.

The Autism Spectrum

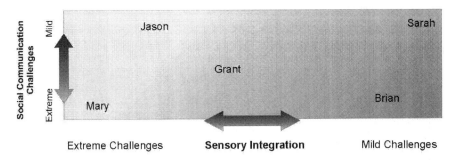

Having splinter skills means that we can have real challenges in one or more areas of life while possessing average or even exceptional abilities in other areas. While most people tend to have certain skills or areas in their lives where they excel relative to other areas of life, these splinter skills can be more pronounced for people on the autism spectrum.

For example, one person might not know how to start or keep a conversation going but can write complex computer programs. Another person might be able to express their thoughts, ideas and feelings eloquently in writing, but freeze up and not be able to speak during a face-to-face conversation. Splinter skills can be hard to recognize. For example, we might be very capable of noticing and talking about subtleties in food or literature but not understand subtleties in human interactions leading to confusion when other people act unpredictably.

Case Study: Joey

Joey is 25. He loves to cook and can accurately describe the recipes he makes with words like "tangy", "pungent", "buttery", "fiery", and "flavorful". Joey likes books almost as much as he loves to cook and he is happy to share his latest read with you. He might even talk about the science fiction novel he is writing about "the intense internal torment that propels Mynar to self destructive tendencies". When talking with Joey, you would never guess he has recently been fired from his job for not following through on directives or that he never buys his favorite vegetable- cucumber, because he does not want to be startled by the mist that keeps the vegetables fresh.

Tip
Rather than trying to determine if we are "high functioning" or "low functioning" and placing us into one of these two categories, find out what our specific splinter skills are.

I can make this . . .

Author photo

Author photo

Handcrafted jewelry

but I can NOT make this . . .

ATM Withdrawal

Check for Splinter Skills

Exercise #1
Part 1:

Make a list of five talents, skills, traits and/or abilities that you know someone on the spectrum has.

#1

_____

#2

_____

#3

_____

#4

_____

#5

_____

(Part 1 can include things like- good with puzzles, knows a lot about geography, doesn't give up, reliable, honest. Feel free to include anything you like about this person).

I can read this . . .

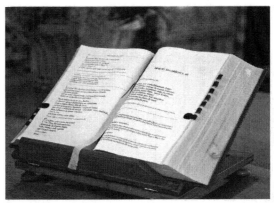

But I can NOT read this . . .

Check for Splinter Skills

Exercise #1
Part 2:

Make a list of five specific challenges that this person faces.

If you don't know and they can tell you, ask them.

#1

_____

#2

_____

#3

_____

#4

_____

#5

_____

(Part 2 can include things like- needs support with: money management, having conversations, saying things tactfully, being in crowds, talking on the phone, dating, hygiene. This list can include things that this person does that irritate or worry you).

Part 3: Now check for splinter skills in your own life. Perhaps you have a successful career but have no idea how to go about dating, or maybe you manage your money well but eat the entire carton of ice-cream or watch too much television, or you take really good care of your children and your spouse but neglect your own needs?

I can navigate this . . .

But I can NOT navigate this . . .

What Happened to Asperger's?

The "official diagnosis" of autism no longer includes Asperger's as a category. Many people choose to continue to use the words "Asperger's", "Aspie" and "Aspergian" anyway because these terms create a useful distinction for those individuals who tend to have specific defining characteristics including average or above average IQ, relatively strong language skills and intense special interests. So while there is no longer an official diagnosis of Asperger's, the term is still used in causal conversations for clarification and as way to self- identify.

Diversity on the Spectrum

Just as ice cream is ice cream whether it is vanilla, chocolate or pistachio, there are as many "flavors" of autism as there are people who are autistic.

You will find people living quiet, uncomplicated lives and you will find noisy, dramatic, high profile and controversial personalities on the spectrum too. We may live in big houses with maids, or little run down trailers in the country. We may drive fast expensive cars, ride the bus or stay locked inside our houses.

We generally like to "do things". We contribute to our communities as postal carriers, janitors, doctors, college professors, grocery clerks, x-ray technicians, librarians, computer programmers, artists, parents, engineers, scientists, assembly line workers, bankers, pet sitters and writers. And yes, we are your friends and neighbors.

Some of us learn to adapt fairly well. Those of us who do, live in-dependently may just stand out from the crowd as "unusual", "eccentric", "insensitive and uncaring" or perhaps having "poor bedside manners". Marcus is a successful administrator at a small college. He shared his personal discoveries after attending an autism training:

Case Study: Marcus

I have always managed to get by alright in my life. I am married, have two children who have left the nest and have cut back my hours to part time because that works for me right now. People have often told me that I was insensitive or uncaring. I don't mean to be that way. So I started thinking that maybe I am an aspergian. Now that I have gone through a training on autism I am fairly certain of it. I don't need to get an official diagnosis. Just knowing for myself helps me understand some of the challenges I have had understanding other people throughout my life.

While Marcus has manged to get along fairly successfully in his life, this is of course not always the case. It is possible to have tremendous gaps in the ability to understand the world and navigate successfully in it. When this happens, comprehensive supports in one or more areas of our lives may be needed and when this is not available, we can experience confusion, social, physical, economic and legal consequences. Jean in the case study below received a late diagnosis of autism and a related genetic condition known as "triple X".

Case Study: Jean

I need a lot of help. I need help when I go to the doctor, if I am signing a lease or any other paperwork and I need help understanding what other people tell me.

When I was a kid I remember walking around in the middle of the street and the other kids were making fun of me but I did NOT know that is what they were doing. My brain didn't get it until later when my brother said "Hey those guys were picking on you."

I didn't understand that there was a difference between boys and girls until I was an adult. I just thought everyone was the same. My teachers had to tell me to take a shower and brush my teeth because my mom didn't know to tell me to do those things.

I didn't realize that I had to work a certain number of hours to be able to make enough money to pay the bills every month and there were times when I had no place to live so people took me in.

Rigid Filters

It is natural for humans to categorize places, people, things and experiences according to similarities. This discrimination helps us filter through massive amounts of information without getting stuck or bogged down so we can focus on what is different or important in any given situation. When filters are based on inaccurate assumptions however, the conclusions are also going to be inaccurate. This often happens when people try to understand autism.

> **Myth**
> I can tell just by looking if a person is autistic.

> **Fact**
> Autism may be noticeable in some people but it is not always obvious as there is a wide range of characteristics that can show up differently in each person.

Having one or two characteristics of autism does not necessarily mean a person is autistic. For example, just because a person spins in circles, does not make eye contact with other people or is hyper-lexic (reads at a very early age) does not necessarily mean they are autistic.

Likewise, just because a person is missing an autistic trait does not necessarily mean that this person is not autistic. Trained evaluators gather early childhood history, make direct observations (sometimes in more than one setting) and use very specific tools before making a diagnosis of autism or ruling it out.

Obsessions & Special Interests

If you ask most people on the spectrum what defines them, they will bring up their special interests. Obsessions may include specialized activities or topics such as watching a fish tank or hamster run around, copying "Sponge Bob" movie credits in a notebook, disassembling electronics or collecting batteries and pens. Special interests may also include general themes like gaming, reading, weather, culture, music sports and cars or trains.

These interests may remain constant through life or change over time. What separates them from the "average" interest is the degree of time and effort spent on these obsessions and/or the uniqueness of the obsession(s).

Case Study: Gavin

When was a kid, I had a thing for batteries and rubber bands. I HAD to collect them. Every day I would search through the drawers and rummage through the house to find them. I had a box for my rubber bands and carried the batteries in my pocket. I could not leave the house until I had at least one battery in both pant pockets. One day my mom cleaned out my room and threw away my rubber band collection. I was crushed. It felt like someone had died. I didn't understand it at the time but those rubber bands represented my security. They were soothing to me the way a parent is soothing to a hurt child.

Tip
Do not get into power struggles over obsessions. Instead, use these unique interests as the starting place to build skills and explore other interests.

Creativity and Humor

The existence or absence of humor is an excellent example of a single characteristic that people often mistakenly use to decide if a person is autistic or not. Many people are under the impression that it's not possible to be autistic and be funny or creative at the same time. Nothing could be further from the truth.

It is true that *some* of us are not creative and don't have a sense of humor. Lack of creativity or humor is not however a requirement for autism. Many of us do develop outlets to express ourselves in unique and funny ways. We can be artists, writers, musicians and actors. And because our brains function differently and we have unique perspectives we are often the very people who develop new ideas, theories and products.

> **Myth**
> Autistic people cannot have a sense of humor or be creative.

> **Fact**
> Some of us are very creative. It is possible to be autistic and have a sense of humor too.

Chris who was diagnosed autistic as a child responds to the notion that people on the spectrum can't have a sense of humor this way: "I find that completely and utterly hilarious!" Not only is Chris able to see humor in given circumstances, he is described by family and friends as "hysterically funny and witty" and "hands down one of the funniest people I have ever known".

Case Study: Jeremiah

I do have an unusual sense of humor and sometimes people don't realize I am joking with them because I am very dead pan when I joke. I laugh about things that other people don't think are funny at all. They just don't get it. For example, Phil Schwartz says that his "Broca's and Wernicke's areas work in Henry James sized quanta, but unfortunately the world has an Ernest Hemingway sized attention span." That is funny to me but I haven't found many people who share my opinion.

Exercise #2: Have a Conversation About Humor

The following questions can get you started:

- ✔ What makes you laugh?
- ✔ What kinds of things do you think are funny?
- ✔ Do you think you have a good sense of humor?
- ✔ Why or why not?

Excelling in One or Many Areas

We often have perfectionist tendencies. This drive for perfection can cause us to get "stuck" on certain topics or tasks, but this hyper focus and our ability to see things from new and unusual perspectives can be an advantage as it often creates the necessary foundation for us to excel in subjects or skills that we find interesting and personally rewarding.

Case Study: Asperger Experts

Danny Raede and Hayden Mears are two young men diagnosed with Asperger's who partnered up for their successful company aspergerexperts.com. They help families deal with the challenges of Asperger's based on their own experiences of what has worked for them. They have a large on-line following and have developed practical programs that work when more traditional approaches have failed. Hayden writes about their mission.

It's a passion project created by those who experienced first hand how difficult and discouraging living with Asperger's can be. It's a promise to create something fulfilling and enriching for other people with Asperger's and their struggling families. It's a dedication to betterment, to happiness, and to living the life you've always craved, regardless of how your brain works."

Case Study: Patrick Jasper Lee

Patrick "Jasper" Lee is probably most known for his unique statements about autism along with his books steeped in Romani culture and mysticism. But the author also paints and composes ethnic music. His books can be found at patrickjasperlee.com.

Case Study: Penelope Trunk

Penelope Trunk is an American business woman who to date has created four start up companies and has a successful business blog. She was a professional beach volleyball player, went to grad school for English and is proficient in HTML. She can be found on-line at penelopetrunk.com where she has plenty of funny things to say about Asperger's and life in general.

Eye Contact

One of the biggest myths about autism is that people on the spectrum don't make eye contact and that anyone who does make eye contact can not be autistic.

> **Myth**
> Autistic people do not make eye contact.

> **Fact**
> Some of us don't make eye contact. Some of us make "good" eye contact and some of us may stare so intensely that other people feel uncomfortable. Eye contact can vary drastically based on circumstances and is a skill that can improve with age.

Case Study: Shawn

Shawn is 24 and has very engaging eye contact. But this wasn't always the case. He went through intensive therapy and credits his speech therapist and psychiatrist for helping him learn how to make eye contact when he was diagnosed with autism at age 7.

It is true that limited eye contact is a common autistic trait but autism and eye contact are not mutually exclusive. One study done in 2006 actually showed that some people on the spectrum may look at faces as much or more than non- autistic people in certain circumstances. We just might be focusing on something different. Many of us look at the mouth, the neck or the ear instead of your eyes.

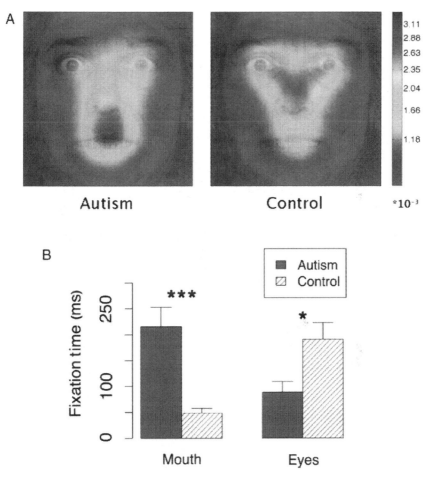

A

Autism   Control   *10⁻³

B

Reprinted with permission[1]

1 Neumann D, Spezio ML, Piven J, & Adolphs R (2006). Looking you in the mouth: abnormal gaze in autism resulting from impaired top-down modulation of visual attention. *Social cognitive and affective neuroscience, 1* (3), 194-202

Eye contact is a skill that improves with age for many of us or may vary from one circumstance to another depending on many factors including:

- ✓ how well we know the person
- ✓ how comfortable we are in the environment
- ✓ what demands are being placed on us
- ✓ how we feel at the time

Quantum Changes Over Time

Nowhere in the official definition of autism does it say that people on the spectrum can't change or adapt to circumstances, but this is a common misconception. Change and adaptation may take time and effort but growth, change and adaptation are absolutely possible.

Myth
Autistic people remain relatively static. They don't change much from one circumstance to another and they don't change much over time.

Fact
We may function very comfortably and effectively in some environments and fall apart in other others. Over time our abilities, skills and personalities can change dramatically. We may make major improvements in our ability to cope in our teens or early adulthood.

Our parents often report that as we grow up we have long periods of time where we remain unchanged followed by bursts of progress in skills and understanding that can best be described as quantum leaps.

<u>Case Study: Diana</u>

When Diana turned 18 she told me "Mom, I'm really surprised you decided to have any more kids after me. I was so crabby and difficult." Diana isn't one to exaggerate.

We soon realized being born on her due date was a prophetic sign of her absolute adherence to being on time and a rigid accuracy in all matters of her life. We brought her home from the hospital where she cried non-stop for three hours, had a seizure, slept it off and promptly started crying again. The only time Diana wasn't crying the first six months of her life was when she slept and when her dad and I bounced her vigorously while jogging through the house. We were completely exhausted. We didn't take Diana to public places until she turned 9 because these excursions always resulted in temper tantrums and inevitable misery for innocent bystanders and us.

But Diana has developed coping skills over time. She is now able to identify when she is anxious or angry and she can talk about it. Some concepts and skills like filtering and prioritizing ideas took her brother and classmate a few minutes to learn but have taken years of persist effort on her part.

"I'm different now." She says. "I think it is because I didn't make excuses not to do things. If I was anxious about something, I decided I'd better face that. So now, I have better coping skills and things just don't upset me as much."

And she is right. Perhaps the best example is how Diana chose to handle her fear of speaking in public. Instead of avoiding circumstances where she would have to speak in front of others, she signed up for a speech class in high school.

Different environments can have an influence on how well we are able to function. There are some of us who do relatively well in the classroom because it is fairly structured and predictable. We might be able to sit comfortably, pay attention and participate successfully when called on but we may also feel overwhelmed in the crowded halls, gymnasiums and the noisy lunch room and find ourselves shutting down in these challenging environments which are not so predictable and structured.

Others of us can sit still in classes that challenge us but if a subject is too difficult, easy or boring we might shut down.

Oftentimes, what we lack in our natural abilities to understand certain ideas is made up for in our sheer persistence and willingness to keep trying. The determination that causes a young autistic child to obsess about light switches or coniferous trees can also be there to help them figure out their world and tenaciously navigate it as they grow up.

It may take much longer to comprehend certain concepts or cultivate skills because we do not develop as quickly or in the same way as people who are not autistic. It may take as much as five or ten extra years before certain ideas make sense.

Tip
Teach us about our changing bodies and setting personal boundaries the same way you taught us how to tie our shoes; step by step, using visual supports and repetition.

Growing Up: Adolescence and Adulthood

Adolescence can be either a time of great strides or extreme difficulty. We may acquire more language and social skills as teenagers and have an easier time in school. Or we might regress during this time and require added patience and support to get through the hormonal changes and other adjustments of growing up.

Tolerance of noises, touch, smells and tastes may decrease during this time or fade away depending on the person. Typically as we move into adulthood we become less rigid. We have had more life experiences and perhaps enough patterns have developed for us to start to understand concepts we had previously struggled with. We have also had opportunities to experiment with and find coping skills that work. Any time there is a change or stressful circumstance in our lives however, we may resort to our previous, more rigid methods of interacting with the world.

Case Study: Amanda

People used to think I was anti-social. I guess in some ways I am, because I like to spend a LOT of time alone. When I was going to school, I couldn't wait to get home every day so I could go to my room and turn on my music. I wouldn't come out until my mom called me for dinner and I would get really upset and yell at her if dinner was early. Now that I'm an adult I kind of get how overwhelmed I used to be with all the sensory stuff at school and the reason I would stay in my room by myself was so I could wind down. I also don't blame myself for feeling so crabby about changes in my routine either because I really needed that down time to recover from all the stimuli of the day but I just don't need that as much now.

I'm really into music. For example, since I got my new iPod last Christmas, I've listened to "Say" by John Mayer 1169 times and "Comatose" by Skillet 1534 times. I've recently started collecting Gregorian Chants and I can tell you the lyrics, length of each song, the choir and producer of each chant. I have all my CD's organized alphabetically in my room with their spines lined up perfectly straight. I get really annoyed if someone accidentally knocks them out of their alignment even just a millimeter. I have always been that way about my things.

I never got an "official diagnosis" of autism but when I got on-line and read about other people who have autism, I just knew. Wow! These people 'get' me! They didn't think it was strange that I only like to eat white rice, peanut butter and chicken nuggets (but only the ones from Chick-fil-A) and I can't stand to have different kinds of food touch each other on the plate. For the first time in my life I felt like someone could understand what I'm going through.

Case Study: Mike

Mike was always a quirky child. His teachers often came to me with concerns about his ability to interact with the other kids. We thought maybe he had ADHD because he had trouble concentrating and sitting still in class but he was a good sweet boy for the most part so we didn't worry too much. I guess I figured he would grow out of it eventually.

When he turned 13, all of that changed overnight. I thought "what happened to my sweet little boy? He has been replaced by some violent stranger". He started getting really upset over little things and ramming his shoulder into the wall on a regular basis. Sometimes he would dent or break the wall with his shoulder or his head. He would pace around talking to himself and rub his cheek until it literally was raw. He started staying up all night. It was like he didn't need to sleep.

We took him to a psychiatrist and we began the search for a medication that would help. Some medications worked like a miracle for a week or two and then he would regress and sometimes get worse. Then the strangest thing happened. I ran into a woman in the store and we just started talking about Mike. She said she had a son with autism that reminded her of him. I was desperate so I went home and spent all night on-line researching autism. I didn't know for sure if that was what was going on but we got him evaluated and sure enough he was diagnosed with autism.

I would be lying if I told you everything got easier at that point. Mike really struggled for the next four years with obsessive thoughts and the need to repeatedly bang his shoulder up against the wall. He especially obsessed about his body parts and whether or not they were normal. He started worrying about his nose and then his genitalia. He is now 19 and he has started to slowly mellow out. Things aren't perfect but his dad and I can definitely see improvements in his ability to sit still and sleep better at night. Something else I've recently noticed is his ability to think about complex topics in school. That is a new skill for him.

Experimentation and Maturity

While autistic males and females tend to develop physically at the same rate as their non-autistic peers, they may take longer to develop emotionally. This can present serious misunderstandings and complications in adolescence and adulthood.

A teenager may be functioning at an emotional age of 8 or 9 and yet be physically, hormonally and sexually sixteen. Connie talks about how this has caused problems for her son.

Case Study: Don

When Don turned 16 we noticed he was still very immature, like an eight year old, but he was also experiencing the normal hormonal thing that boys go through. The problem was that he was not interested in girls his own age. He was interested in girls much younger. Fortunately we had a really good therapist at the time who had worked with other boys on the spectrum and she was able to help me understand that he was attracted to younger girls because they matched his maturity level, and he felt safe around them, not because he had some sort of deviant problem. She gave him very specific training on sexuality and he responded really well to learning the rules of what he could and could not do.

This was fourteen years ago and Don's emotional maturity has caught up with him but in hindsight, if it wasn't for having the therapist recognize and deal with Don's needs head on, I think we could have been headed for some serious problems.

Relationships

We may need more time in solitude to recharge but very few of us actually prefer complete isolation. As a matter of fact, many of us long for human contact and feel lonely when we don't have meaningful inter-actions with other people.

Myth
Autistic people are not interested in relationships.

Fact
Many of us are very interested in having friendships and or romantic relationships and families. We don't always know how to achieve our relationship goals, we may get easily discouraged and give up or you may not feel comfortable knowing how to do your part to further the interaction along.

Mick shares his feelings of isolation and disappointment about a recent event where he hoped to make friends.

Case Study: Mick

Maybe I saw the Doctor Who event as an opportunity to meet some-one new. But then when it didn't go as planned then I might have become kind of shocked because of the vulnerability and because of that I couldn't see any other way to meet any new persons in real life. I am kind of lonely at this very moment.

Handshakes, Hugs and Sex

It is important to recognize that many of us do not feel comfortable with certain kinds of physical contact, and we appreciate when you take the time and effort to find out what we are comfortable with before initiating any kind of touch. But many autistic people do enjoy and seek out specific types of physical contact.

Myth
Autistic people don't like to be touched and therefore don't want to have any physical contact with other people.

Fact
While some people on the spectrum do not want to have physical contact with others, there are many of us who do want to connect physically with people. It all depends on the individual.

Case Study: Jeremiah

I have always had a healthy expression of my sexuality and enjoy giving hugs and holding my wife's hand. The aspect I needed help with when I was younger was learning to read the cues and knowing when someone I was interested in was also interested in me. I was that annoying teenage boy who would try to hold a girl's hand or kiss her before she was ready or even when she wasn't interested at all and I had to learn the hard way that physical contact needs to be mutually agreed upon. I still don't read my wife's moods well and we have been together now for 14 years.

She has to make it a point to tell me if she needs a hug or wants her space. I am told that other husbands are able to know these things just by observing.

Case Study: Greg

I feel that I am ready to embark on a new stage with my girlfriend. We have been together for 6 months. We both have Asperger's and we have a trusting relationship but I have not kissed her yet. I do not know how to kiss someone and she doesn't either so we don't know where to begin. We may need a training to help us.

Tip

If we are able to tell you, then ask us what kind of physical contact we are comfortable with before touching us. If we are unable to communicate this for any reason find out from someone who knows us well.

Case Study: Amanda

I have always been sort of OK with giving my mom hugs. As I have gotten older I have learned to give hugs to my dad and my friends too. It depends on the day but sometimes hugs don't feel that good and so I prefer when people ask me if they can give me a hug first. Something else that bothers me is if someone comes up behind me and gives me a hug. It kind of startles me and I can't mentally prepare if I don't see it coming.

Case Study: Judy

I had sex for the first time when I was 21. I didn't know what it was supposed to be like and I thought that if I just took some time and got used to it certain things would stop hurting if I kept doing them. Then a friend told me that I need to let my boyfriend know if something feels uncomfortable so he can do things differently and I can be comfortable.

Women and Autism

There is very little research regarding women and autism. What we do know is:

- ✓ For every female who receives an official autism diagnosis, 4 males are diagnosed.

- ✓ New studies are addressing the possibility that autism may show up in males differently than it does in females. In other words testing for autism may not accurately identify the presence of autism in females and they may be under-diagnosed.

- ✓ Females with IQ's below 70 tend to function lower than males but we do not see this same pattern when women have higher IQ's[2].

- ✓ Special interests for females may be considered more "socially appropriate" and therefore not easily recognized as "perseverative".

---

2 Frazier T.W. *et al. J. Am. Acad. Child Adolesc. Psychiatry* **53**, 329-340 (2014)

Emma discussed her own autism and her observation of other women in the comment section of an on-line article about women and autism.

Case Study: Emma

I firmly believe . . . that it is just harder to spot in females. Mainly because they seem better at identifying and then compensating for their social difficulties. However what I have observed is that the traits become most pronounced when these females are under pressure. Anxiety, depression, emotional breakdown and social withdrawal result. I agree females are much less likely to have unusual social interests, they are most definitely there though. I also believe that although women and girls can appear to cope better than males, the continual exertion required to cope with social situations leave women exhausted. At high school I began to develop migraines. I got a migraine every Friday. Whenever I engage in demanding social situations, I am exhausted afterwards.[3]

---

3 Autism Characteristics Differ by Gender, Studies Find
   https://spectrumnews.org/news/autism-characteristics-differ-by- gender-studies-fnd/
   by Sarah Deweerdt 3/27/2014

Exercise #3: The following screening tool is based on feedback from women who are self-identified or have received a formal diagnosis of autism. The greater number of "yes" responses, the greater likelihood that autism may be a factor in this person's life. This tool is most suitable for verbal females 11 years and older.

While not meant to diagnose, this tool can help females decide if they should investigate the possibility of autism further.

Autism Screening Tool for Girls and Women

Circle each of the boxes next to any question you answer "yes" to for you or someone you know.

Do you or someone you know:

- ☑ Become exhausted after social interactions that don't seem to tire other people (e.g. have unusually low energy after a day at school, family gathering or holiday. This may show up as calling in sick or canceling plans)?

- ☑ Study human behaviors and interactions in detail so that you can model or copy them in your own life (e.g. through movies, read books and/or observe people)?

- ☑ Get upset when others do not use reason or logic?

- ☑ Become very critical over things that other people don't even seem to notice such as discrepancies in movies, a poorly designed system, or sloppy paint job?

- ☑ Explore an interest to a greater degree than most people so that you become an expert or excel in one or more areas, fields or topics?

- ☑ Have sensitivities to sights sounds, smells, tastes or touch that do not bother other people?

- ☑ Does this sensitivity get worse during times of sickness and/or stress?

- Are you under-sensitive to certain sensations that cause other people discomfort (e.g. burns, scrapes, cuts, don't realize you broke a bone, or sit calmly through labor pains)?

- Do you need more time than most people in solitude to recharge?

- Do changes in your routine and/or the method or order in which you do things upset you (e.g. an unannounced visitor shows up at your house, your ride home needs to make a detour, an unexpected invitation to a pleasurable activity)?

- Do you stick to a routine even when shortcuts or a different route might be faster or better (e.g. walk to school the same way, park in the same place, walk down aisles in a certain order at the grocery store even when you don't need items in these aisles)?

- Do you become more upset with changes in your routine when you are in a stressful or unpredictable circumstance?

- Do you have strong visual skills and/or think in pictures? Do images pop into your head?

- Do you see, hear, smell, taste, or feel sensations that other people do not?

- Have you made decisions in your life based on observing someone else's choices (e.g. get married or choose a certain career) without considering important factors such as relationship compatibility or ability to perform required job duties?

- For younger women and girls, do you dress up in costumes and or play roles in social settings based on what you see in movies, books magazines or real life in order to fit in?

- Have you remained in an untenable situation (e.g. abusive/unhealthy romantic relationship or friendship, job, living situation) when other people would have left because you did not think you had another alternative and/or because you were determined to make it work?

- Do you have a hard time understanding how other people in your life might not have the same moral or ethical codes as you when it comes to relationships or honesty (e.g. have a hard time believing someone would lie to you, cheat or steal from you or manipulate you)?

- Do you look at the mouth, neck or shoulders instead of the eyes when talking to people and/or find eye contact to be uncomfortable or painful?

- Do you refuse to give up on a project or relationship long after other people would have quit?

- Do you delay or completely avoid certain projects or responsibilities that other people have no trouble completing because you have no idea how to begin them or need extra time to process how to proceed?

- Do you have children, siblings or other relatives diagnosed with autism?

- Is your language more formal or more precise than most people's and/or do you catch yourself simplifying your vocabulary so that others will understand you?

- Do you lack the ability to correctly interpret some or all subtle or symbolic gestures or signs (e.g. don't know how to tell if someone has a crush, wants to be friends or feels hostile towards you, can't tell when people are bored or need to leave)?

- Do you have difficulty maintaining work or school attendance, staying employed or are you under-employed?

- Do other people have unrealistic expectations of you because of your intelligence (e.g. they say things like "you are too smart for that job")?

- Do you feel emotions less and/or more intensely or differently than most people?

- Do you frequently notice patterns in things (e.g. visual, behavioral, numerical)?

- Do you create systems or groups to help you understand situations and/or functions?

- Do you have difficulty stopping an activity once you get started (e.g. clean the whole house, fix a computer glitch or finish an entire homework assignment without taking a break. May regularly skip meals, drinks and bathroom breaks and/or go for unusually long periods of time to fix something, finish a project or research a subject)?

- Do you feel more comfortable with people who are younger and older than people your own age?

- Do you have unusual or excessive fears or anxieties (e.g. talking on the telephone, dolls, mirrors)?

- Do you often say things that other people feel are rude, embarrassing or inappropriate though it is not your intention to be hurtful?

- Do you feel uncomfortable interacting with other people (e.g. not know what to say, how to hold your posture, make gestures and/or facial expressions)?

- Do you sometimes pretend to understand what other people say or do so that you won't call attention to yourself?

- Do you worry to an unusual degree about something that might happen or do you have trouble letting go of things that don't seem to bother other people?

- Do you find it unacceptable when others violate established rules (e.g. a friend wants to play a board game using new rules, drives 5 miles over the speed limit or crosses in the middle of the street instead of at the crosswalk)?

Putting it All Into Perspective

Autism can show up in many different ways. Because of the inherent nature of splinter skills and our ability to develop coping strategies it may actually be hard to recognize that some people are on the spectrum until you get to know them very well and see how they handle a variety of circumstances.

Rather than trying to pigeonhole someone into a "high" or "low" functioning category, it makes more sense to discover what our specific splinter skills are and provide needed support and understanding based on those areas where we feel challenged. It is possible to be autistic and:

✔ have a good sense of humor
✔ be creative
✔ excel in one or many areas
✔ make eye contact
✔ change, adapt and develop coping skills over time
✔ be interested in having friends and/or romantic relationships
✔ enjoy physical contact

Adolescents may encounter difficulties adjusting to hormonal and social changes. As a result, adolescence can be a very challenging time. In some instances however, these hormonal shifts actually have the opposite effect and life becomes more manageable.

Females can experience autism differently than males. They tend to develop more effective coping strategies in some cases and their obsessive interests are considered to be more socially acceptable. As a result, many women may go undiagnosed because evaluators are trained to identify characteristics of autism that are associated with men. They may not pick up on feminine examples of the criteria for autism.

So whatever happened to Martha? She finally found a new apartment not too far from her job with a landlord who was understanding of her situation. She received staff support twice a week to help her balance her checkbook and deal with personal issues like interacting with her neighbors. Martha was very eager to learn new ways to interact with people and quickly caught on to money management skills.

Once her splinter skills were recognized and addressed Martha was able to develop positive relationships with her neighbors.

Martha never talked about her parents. But when she moved into her new place I helped her hang a black and white picture of a woman who bore a strong resemblance to her above the mantle.

Martha remained content in her new home until she died peacefully at age 76 almost 20 years after we initially met. I am told that the neighbor who lived next door sat by her side till the end and I like to think that the woman whose picture I hung up all those years ago, whoever she was, would have been pleased to know that Martha lived a safe, happy and peaceful life.

To Do List

_____Exercise #1: Check for Splinter Skills *(pg 15)*

      _____Part 1: Identify Talents, Skills, Strengths and Abilities

      _____Part 2: Identify Areas where Support is Needed

      _____Part 3: Identify Splinter Skills in your own Life *(pg 17)*

_____Exercise #2: Have a Conversation With Me About Humor *(pg 24)*

_____Exercise #3: For femles who suspect they might be autistic *(pg 39)*
"Autism Screening Tool for Girls and Women"

Autism really can be a gift if you learn to live with it. It's kinda like X-men with their superpowers.
Mick Prangsbøll

What is normal?
Sue Taylor

Key # 2
"Problem" Alchemy
Turn Troubles into Strengths

*I*n fifth grade Diana walked in the house with a history assignment. She promptly sat down at the desk and answered the first two questions. Twenty minutes later, she was still stumped on question number three.

I looked over her shoulder. Questions one, two and four were easy. The answers were concrete and stated verbatim in her textbook. Question three was abstract and required Diana to make some complicated inferences. "That question is hard. Why don't you do question four and come back to it later?" I innocently recommended.

"I can't!" She whined, stomped her feet, threw her head back and growled. Yes, she growled. It was her usual sign of frustration, a ritual she repeated many times each day to the constant dread of everyone else in the house.

Diana spent two and a half hours on that history assignment. It probably took the other kids in her class no more than 20 minutes.

Something about the way her brain was hardwired would not let her skip that question and come back to it later. She HAD to answer the questions in order.

We were always on guard for the next crisis- the next unanswerable history question or innocent comment that would instigate a meltdown. I wondered how this cranky child was going to navigate through middle school and then the rest of her life when she was unable to get through ten minutes at a restaurant or the grocery store without having a meltdown.

Her younger brother perceptively commented, "I don't think it is going to turn out well when Diana decides to get a boyfriend." It was easy at the time to look at these incidents through a magnifier to see how difficult life was for everyone involved and assume it was going to be that way FOREVER. But it wasn't forever.

Diana is in college now. She reports that during tests she answers the easy questions first then returns to the more challenging ones.

Somewhere between fifth grade and adulthood she acquired this useful strategy. The noisy, aggressive, hand flapping child who had me questioning whether she would even graduate from high school didn't just graduate- she did it with honors while working a part time job and mentoring other young people who are autistic. But that isn't the point of this story.

I could say: "Thank goodness Diana has learned how to skip questions and come back to them later!" "Thank goodness she got over that annoying obsession with blood and gore." "Thank goodness I don't have to put groceries on the conveyor belt 'the right way' anymore" and "Thank goodness I can freely estimate the time now without being corrected with "It's not 7:30 mom. It is 7:32." But I won't.

I won't dismiss these things as annoyances because the successes in Diana's life are actually in large part a result of the same stubborn determination, stick-to-it-ness and quirky obsessions that put her on the autism spectrum in the first place. Let me say that again. Diana's successes in life are NOT in spite of her autistic characteristics, they are BECAUSE of her autistic characteristics.

Diana is studying nursing. It is a career ideally suited to her unique and quirky traits. Her childhood obsession with gore has mellowed into the ability to regard blood, cuts, sores and other medical conditions with mild curiosity, while her classmates are growing queasy or passing out next to her.

When she was little, she was overwhelmed in stores because she saw and heard all the little details that no one else even noticed. But today, observing small but important changes in a patient's condition and accurately documenting vital signs and medication doses are skills that Diana will have no trouble exercising in her chosen career.

Diana likes to follow the rules. As a child she couldn't do question number four until she had completed question number three because in her mind, that was the "rule." Diana will have the ability to consistently follow infection control protocol step by step because her brain is comfortable sticking to the rules when other people might get bored and sloppy with the same routine.

From the time Diana was about 9 she started having "imaginary conversations" with people. She created hypothetical scripts between herself and people she wanted to communicate a particular idea to. Perhaps she wanted to ask a teacher to explain an idea differently so she could understand it better or tell a friend she didn't feel like hanging out. She spent about 10 hours a week on these hypothetical conversations.

To those of us who listened to the same script 50 times in an hour this was a lesson in patience but Diana was actually putting neuroscience to work for her. This repetitive language in the form of role playing is actually proven to be especially effective in decreasing anxiety and accomplishing goals.

Diana's ability to harness her autistic traits punctuates one of the biggest misunderstandings about autism.

> **Myth**
> Autistic characteristics are inherently negative. In order to support someone on the spectrum, I should help them get rid of these traits so that they can be more "normal".

Autism and Self-Identity

While therapists, doctors and parents of young children often refer to autism as a "disease", "disability" or "tragedy", an overwhelming majority of adults on the spectrum have a very different idea.

Case Study: Vince

If someone decided that because descendants from Africa have a greater genetic disposition towards sickle cell anemia that we should cure being "black" they would be considered prejudiced and illogical. Rightly so. We chose to treat the sickle cell instead.

Likewise, just because an autistic person has a greater probability of dealing with gastro-intestinal problems for example, does not mean that getting rid of autism is the solution. This idea ranks right up there with lobotomizing patients in the 40's.

I have no interest in being "cured" or "fixed" and I find it ironic that those of us on the spectrum are accused of rigid thinking when so many neurotypical notions of autism can be only described as just that, "rigid". For example, I find it rigid thinking to assume the autistic brain is a mistake of nature.

Temple Grandin is credited for saying "Who do you think made the first stone spears? The Asperger guy. If you were to get rid of all the autism genetics, there would be no more Silicon Valley." I agree with this perspective. In my mind it makes more sense to see those of us with autism as part of the diversified whole of the human race.

Autism advocate Jim Sinclair describes the inextricable link between autism and self-identity:

> *Autism is a way of being. It is pervasive; it colors every experience, every sensation, perception, thought, emotion, and encounter, every aspect of existence. It is not possible to separate the autism from the person-- and if it were possible, the person you'd have left would not be the same person you started with.*

As an autistic synaethete, Author Patrick Jasper Lee often experiences the universe and people in it as shapes. He believes that this unusual way to perceive the world gives him an advantage when communicating and relating to the natural world. He gently pokes fun at the idea that he has a "condition" that should be "cured":

> *The world has a fast-growing problematic disability, which forges bonds in families, causes people to communicate in direct and clear ways, cuts down meaningless social interaction, pushes people to the limit with learning about themselves, whilst making them work together to make a better world. It's called Autism-- and I can't see anything wrong with it, can you? Boy I'm glad I also have this disability!*

This concept of acceptance is simple yet profound. It turns the medical model of autism treatment over on its head. Instead of finding a remedy or a cure for hand flapping, obsessive conversations and poor eye contact, therapists, teachers and other supporters can search for ways to harness and utilize these same characteristics to promote learning, friendship and employment the same way Diana has chosen a career that plays to her autistic strengths.

Exercise #4: Re-frame "Problems" as Strengths

Make a list of the five most troublesome characteristics that concern you about someone you know on the spectrum and re-frame them as possible strengths:

"Problem":   >   Strength:

#1_____

#2_____

#3_____

#4_____

#5_____

(You can include favorite obsessions such as only talks about "culverts" or "coniferous trees", personality traits such as focusing on little details like a spec of dust or the precise word to describe a color, brutal honesty, or rude comments, sensory behaviors such as rocking back and forth or taking apart video equipment. And for those of you who care about someone who head bangs or smears feces this exercise is still for you!)

When therapy, support and treatment are needed, they can be provided within a framework that supports and accepts autistic characteristics as a gift rather than trying to eliminate this uniqueness just because it is "different". For example:

   ✓   Instead of therapy to eliminating hand flapping provide exposure to activities like painting, basketball, massage, knitting, hanging clothes, rolling paper beads or fixing tires on bikes to capitalize on the natural tendency to keep the hands moving.

✓ Instead of eliminating or ignoring obsessions, use them as motivation and a starting place for therapy and education. As small children, these obsessions can seems very worrisome to parents and other caregivers but as we get older, these same obsessions are often the very motivators we need to accomplish our goals and they may actually open up career opportunities.

✓ Incorporate rocking, spinning or jumping into the beginning of therapy and teaching sessions as a starting place instead of trying to eliminate these behaviors before therapy begins.

✓ Utilize strong visual skills to help eliminate anxiety and accomplish goals by rewiring how the brain thinks and reacts to information through visualization techniques. Research in the field of neuro-science has actually demonstrated that strong visualization skills are effective at reducing anxiety and achieving goals.

Employment Challenges and Advantages

Adults on the spectrum are considerably under employed, but research shows that autistic people actually make excellent employees when placed in jobs that play to our strengths and support us with the right accommodations. We generally are punctual, have good attendance, are detail oriented, good at following the rules, remain focused and do not exploit or steal from our employer or customers.

✓ Would someone who is blatantly honest make a good movie critic or product tester?

✓ Would someone who gets stuck on details make a good technical writer, wine taster or janitor?

✓ Would someone who makes lists all day make a good inventory control person or data technician?

As a matter of fact, autistic employees can cut down significantly on company turn over and improve service and product quality. This can result in increased profits as well as client/customer satisfaction.

Case Study: MeanStream Studios

MeanStream Studios was founded by Producer/Director Hector Salazar to address the needs of mid to large sized companies needing innovative web and multi-media solutions. Many of the individuals he recruits for his team possess unique talents and also happen to be autistic.

His business model and company culture are designed to maximize employee potential and accommodate the needs of these autistic employees. Hector regularly mentors autistic individuals who are exploring multi-media and web design in what he calls a win-win arrangement. MeanStream employees and trainees "think outside the box and bring something original to a project that only they can offer".

His company can be found at Meanstreamstudios.org.

Being autistic can create some unusual challenges that need to be addressed when finding and maintaining a job:

- ✓ Knowing if and when to disclose autism to supervisors and colleagues.

- ✓ Autistics may have a hard time "selling" ourselves in the selection process even when we are the best qualified for the job.

- ✓ Autistic employees may take longer to learn job duties than non-autistic counterparts.

✓ Autistic employees may need specific supports to deal effectively with changes in job duties, supervisors and environment.

✓ Employees on the spectrum may need some accommodations or adjustments in the work environment and how directives are given to perform duties. For example, an employee may need to have all supervisor requests in writing or need to take shorter more frequent breaks than other workers.

✓ Autistic employees may need specific guidance on how to tactfully express opinions, how to interact with colleagues, or learning when to ask for help.

✓ Prospective employees may need support in understanding the effects of employment on disability benefits.

<u>Case Study: Jeff</u>

I stayed home to raise my children but now that my youngest is in school and doing well I need to look for a job. Back in my father's time a person had a career. Nowadays it's normal to have six or seven jobs in a lifetime. I can guarantee that this kind of uncertainty isn't helpful for autistics.

There are a lot of considerations that other people don't have to think about. For example, do I tell people I have a diagnosis of autism during the interview or keep it to myself? And what if part of my job would require an accommodation. Do I talk about that or wait until later?

I had a job once at a fast food restaurant which wasn't good for anybody. If someone ordered a #6 I would say "You don't want that."

And they would say "Yes I do."

I would say, "No, you don't. You should order the #3 instead." Then they would ask why and I'd tell them, "The #6 is no good."

After that job I went to work for a small office as an assistant filing papers and managing behind the scenes. That worked out great for everybody. My boss was really happy with my work and I didn't have the pressure of dealing with the customers.

It really isn't any different for someone with or without autism. Having the right job and an understanding supervisor is key.

Exercise #5: What is Already Working?

Instead of focusing on our differences as "problems" that need to be fixed, ask yourself how these differences are currently working for us or how they can be utilized to improve our:

- ✓ school or career
- ✓ relationships
- ✓ health
- ✓ finances
- ✓ leisure time

Thoughts for Parents of Young Children
With Classic Autism

A few years ago an angry father wrote a post in reaction to an article that highlighted the fact that Daryl Hannah was diagnosed with autism. "No way that she can have autism!" He wrote. "My son has autism and she is nothing like my son." He compared the actress to his 8 year old child who made no eye contact, rarely spoke and rocked non-stop. The father then accused her of "making it up to get attention" and taking the focus away from children who "really need help".

Parents of newly diagnosed or young children often express this kind of frustration, anger and disbelief towards teens and adults with more subtle signs of autism.

We get it. You are dealing with poop smeared on walls, head banging, sleep deprivation, and the risk of losing your job because the school keeps calling you to take your child home for disruptive behaviors, or some combination of problems that are equally painful and exhausting. And to be honest, anyone who doesn't have a child in this circumstance just can't understand what it is like for you.

So what could those of us who drive cars, have jobs and families have in common with your non-verbal child? The answer is our past. Some of us have been where your child is now. Some of us spent our early years in a non-verbal world spinning in circles, flipping light switches, climbing walls and smearing poop just like your child does now and we have simply grown into a new stage where it is easier for us to function and relate to a non-autistic world because we have had a whole lot of practice and have developed good coping skills.

You do not know the quiet desperation, paralyzing anxiety and excruciating pain that marked childhood for many of us. But we do know what it is like for your child to navigate a frightening and unpredictable world because we have been there. You do not know the joy, and simple pleasures of going deeply into the mind where nothing foreign or painful can penetrate. But we do know what it is like for your child to exist in the safety and solitude of their imagination. We have the larger perspective of having changed and grown as a result of our experiences over time.

So instead of judging us because we as are not exactly like your child, let's work together to make things better for all of us. We have already paved a path so you don't have to go it alone.

Putting it All Into Perspective

Many of the habits and behaviors that caregivers find concerning or annoying in autistic children can actually be beneficial for these same children as they grow up. Strict adherence to rules, attention to detail and unwavering repetitive behaviors can be utilized to achieve difficult goals and perform detail oriented tasks.

Most autistic people see autism as an integral part of their identity and don't want to be "fixed". Instead they would like to be accepted and given support in those areas that they find challenging or difficult to manage.

Employees on the spectrum as a general rule make excellent contributions and can increase company profits and service quality when they are

1- in the right job
2- with the right accommodations.

Today when Diana calls home from school it's to let me know how work is going, for input on a writing assignment or to process what she needs to do to take care of her new dog who is potty training.

Some abstract concepts are still difficult for her but in many ways she is more mature at 21 than I was at 38. She sets clear boundaries for herself by limiting the number of hours she is willing to work and and doesn't allow people in her life to cross those boundaries. In contrast, when I was her age I said "yes" to everything. She has her share of challenges but overall Diana is happy and enjoying her independence.

I never could have imagined the young woman she is today who has blossomed from the rigid and irritable five year old who couldn't enter a restaurant without having a meltdown. While no one can predict how any child will progress, we all do grow, learn and develop each in our own unique and often surprising ways.

To Do List

_____Exercise #4: Re-frame "Problems" as Strengths *(pg 54)*

_____Exercise #5: What is Already Working? *(pg 58)*

Autists are the ultimate square pegs and the problem with pounding a square peg into a round hole is not that the hammering is hard work. It's that you're destroying the peg.
Paul Collins

Key # 3
Understand How Sensory Integration & Anxiety Affect My Life

*A*round the time Diana turned ten, we acquired the game Boggle. We all sat down at the dining table and her brother gave the box an innocent shake. Diana jumped up from her chair, squealed "No!" and left the room. For years, any time Boggle appeared at the table, Diana disappeared. The noise hurt her ears. For that matter, coins jingling in someone's pocket, the turntable on the DVD player and her brother's laughter all hurt her ears. We absolutely dreaded the 4th of July. We usually tried to accommodate Diana when she complained that something hurt her ears but I drew the line the day and she told me to stop breathing!

You may have noticed that the standard description of autism includes communication problems first, socialization difficulties second and unusual, repetitive sensory behaviors last. This description is based on the previous "Diagnostic and Statistical Manual Fourth Edition (DSM IV) definition of autism and it is how people typically define autism.

Most interventions and behavioral treatments follow this order by focusing first on improving communication and then socialization skills and limiting or eliminating behaviors such as rocking back and forth, spinning in circles or flipping light switches.

Well guess what! We have been saying for years that this approach is backwards. And not only is this approach backwards, it neglects to address the most important aspect of our sensory experience- how our bodies actually feel.

Diana's refusal to play Boggle wasn't a social problem even though it appeared to be. It was a sensory problem. She was protecting herself by avoiding a painful noise. And this hypersensitivity to sound resulted in her inability to participate in a social activity.

Learning Under Stress

It's a fact. No one learns well or communicates effectively in a state of fight or fight. And that is exactly the position we are in when our sensory system is operating at a heightened state. This heightened awareness of sights, smells, touch, taste and/or sound increases our level of anxiety because our senses feel constantly under attack. Teachers, parents and therapists are busy trying to get us to learn social and communication skills while we are in an anxious and defensive state of mind. But don't take our word for it. Research has shown that when a person learns under conditions of stress, the memory is impaired[4] and the learner may become rigid in their ability to apply this knowledge in their lives favoring "habit" over a more flexible "thought based or cognitive" type of memory[5]. For those of us who are autistic, this rigid type of learning tends to be especially pronounced and so it is very important to create a safe environment for skill development so that we can establish the right pathways in our brain for flexible and adaptive learning.

Here it the good news. Oftentimes when our sensory challenges are addressed, the communication and socialization problems that are important to you become easier to address and sometimes even cease to be problems at all.

---

4 *Learning under stress impairs memory formation.* Neurobiology Learning Memory. 2010 Feb;93(2):183-8. doi: 10.1016/j.nlm.2009.09.009. Epub 2009 Sep 29.
5 *Stress modulates the use of spatial versus stimulus-response learning strategies in humans.* Learning & Memory. 2007 Jan-Feb; 14(1-2): 109–116.

Common Sensory Myths

For most people the daily experience of sensations is like the daily experience of breathing. Not much thought actually goes into the process of "sensing" unless something is out of balance or extraordinary in some way. This has led to some common misunderstandings about the world of the senses in general and specifically about how those of us on the spectrum experience the world around us. The following are some of the most common misunderstandings people have about the senses and how people on the spectrum are affected by them.

Myth
Autistic people experience sight, sound, touch, taste, smell, balance and body awareness "just like everybody else".

Fact
Each of us feels and interprets the same sensory data differently depending how sensitive we are to a given stimulus.

We may experience heightened sensory feedback to our bodies on a regular basis. This can cause confusion, disorientation and even pain in some cases. It is also possible to experience diminished sensations so we are unaffected by events that would cause most people to feel discomfort or pain such as a broken bone or an illness.

People who are oversensitive to specific sounds, touch, taste, sight or smells are referred to as **hypersensitive**. People who do not feel as much as the typical person are referred to as **hyposensitive**. Unfortunately, many people simply dismiss hyper and hyposensitivity, having never experienced it for themselves. Therefore, although it is one of the most important issues to address, it is also one of the least understood aspects of autism and we are offered very little support to cope with it. The new DSM V places more emphasis on the sensory aspect of autism and time will tell how this affects treatment and support.

Case Study: Amanda

I've always had this "problem" with my skin. When I was little, practically everything hurt when it touched me- tags on shirts, jeans, seams in socks, shoes, hats. Even worse was when my mom would try to brush my hair or clip my nails. I remember screaming about that. I would never let people hug or kiss me either because I felt like I couldn't breathe.

When I turned fourteen some of that started to go away and I remember that was a big deal to my mom. I remember her telling everyone "Amanda wears jeans now". Things didn't hurt so much when I turned fourteen but about that time I traded in the pain for an itching problem. Sometimes my skin just itches for no reason, especially my arms and feet and the cold still hurts my skin like when I go into a grocery store or when we have freezing rain.

My parents took me to the doctor when I was twelve, to see what the problem was and he said there was nothing wrong with me. "It's all in her head". After the doctor said that, I started to think maybe I was crazy until I got on line and started meeting other autistic people who could relate to what I have gone through. The thing is, if you spend your whole life being different from everyone else and they tell you that you must be crazy for feeling a certain way, then you start to believe them. Now that I've met other people on the spectrum who have experienced similar things sometimes even worse than what I have been through, I know I'm not crazy, it's just the sensory part of my autism coming out.

You see there is one other thing I would like for people to know. People without autism have a hard time understanding what it is like to do even the simple day-to-day things that they take for granted, like meeting new people for example or going to a new environment.

Exercise #6: Walk in My Shoes

Read the following description and take five minutes to think about it. Imagine how you would feel if you had to face similar challenges in every aspect of your life every single day:

Imagine for a moment, entering a room for the first time for an important job interview. You are "hit" with the noxious smell of something rotting in the refrigerator mixed with an over-powering perfume. You feel like retching. Bright lights shine directly into your eyes so you aren't sure if there are two or three people sitting at the table in front of you.

When you finally feel your way through the disorienting light into a chair, someone asks you a question over the sound of a loud fan, you vaguely hear them say "This   .   .   . highly sought   .   .   .   committee   would.   .   . what qualifications . . . bring . . . candidates?"

You really want this job but you have no idea what the question was and furthermore you are suddenly aware that you squinted your eyes, scrunched your nose up and pulled back abruptly when you entered the room in response to the strong odors and bright light. It was not the first impression you had hoped to make. You reply,"Well, the candidates for this position should be hard working, reliable and creative."

A voice from across the table responds once again over the fan "Yes, but. . . above your . . .competition?"

You are painfully aware that the noise of the fan and the queasy sensation in your stomach prevented you from hearing the question as it was stated: "This is a highly sought after position. The committee would like to know what qualifications you can bring to the job over the other candidates? What sets you above your competition?"

Sensory experiences play a major role in every aspect of life including the ability to function in an environment and relate to other people. If you want to understand what it is like to be autistic, then it is vital to understand this:

> If I am hyper and/or hypo sensitive, this can affect every aspect of my life including my ability to communicate and socialize effectively!

The Hidden Senses

Taste, touch, smell, sight and sound are not the only senses that humans experience. There are two additional senses that affect the ability to function in any given environment.

> **Myth:**
> Humans only have five senses: Taste, touch, sight, smell and sound.

> **Fact:**
> In addition to taste, touch, sight, smell and sound there are two additional senses sometimes called "the hidden senses" or *vestibular* and *proprioceptive* senses.

"Vestibular" refers to our sense of balance that is regulated by the inner ear. It creates the awareness of space, gravity and movement as well as our head and body position in relation to the earth.

"Proprioceptive" refers to our awareness of what our body parts are doing and where they are in relation to the world around us. The muscles, joints and ligaments provide the body with this information.

Body Awareness

Many of us have an unusual sense of how our bodies are in relation to the rest of the world. We may like to stand too close to you and not even realize we are stepping on your toes. Or we may not be able to distinguish between our arm and the chair it is resting on. "Sensory behaviors such as head banging, wearing tight belts or heavy backpacks and squeezing behind the couch are ways to give our bodies the needed feedback to help regulate vestibular and proprioceptive senses.

Communication and the Senses

Margo describes the challenges she experiences when trying to communicate with her husband Jeff who recently discovered that he is autistic.

Case Study: Jeff

Communication sometimes feels impossible because Jeff gets so caught up in seeing and sensing the world around him that he can't stay focused on the subject. One time I came home and he had painted the wall without consulting me and when I asked him "why on earth did you go and paint the wall red without asking me first?" He spent fifteen minutes focusing on the color of the wall, "it's mauve" he said and went into an elaborate demonstration of the finer details between shades of red and mauve. For me, the color of the wall wasn't important, it was the fact that he did something without asking me that I wanted to talk about. I have to remember that this is the way his brain works. It just gets caught up in what he feels or sees, like the color of the wall.

While the traditional approach is to describe this kind of hyper-focus as a "communication problem" which prevents the conversation from moving forward, it is actually helpful to recognize the role that sensory perception plays in how a person's mind gets stuck on what they sense in the first place.

On a positive note, many of us possess an acute awareness of our bodies, the environment and any subtle changes in them. This can be helpful when trying to determine nutrition plans, effective medications or useful therapies. Furthermore, some of us are able to utilize our heightened senses to our advantage in our careers and personal lives.

Emotions

Experts have a hard time agreeing on just exactly what emotions are. For the purpose of our discussion we refer to emotions as "a state of feeling" (e.g. the experiences of happiness, anger, sadness, frustration, contentment, excitement, peacefulness). What experts do agree on is the fact that emotions affect the physical state of our bodies.

And while those of us who are autistic tend to be more comfortable navigating the world based on what makes logical sense, we still experience emotions and these feelings can drastically affect our ability to communicate.

To understand how emotions affect us and influence our interactions it helps to break the emotional experience into three separate parts:

1. how we "feel"
2. our recognition and understanding of these emotions in ourselves and others
3. our ability to talk about these feelings

We may feel some or all of our emotions to a lesser or greater degree than most people or we may feel them differently. We may feel an emotion but not necessarily be able to identify or understand what we are experiencing and we may have a limited ability to talk about these feelings regardless of how we feel them.

Diana as a child for example was able to recognize that she was angry but didn't understand how she ended up in this emotional state until she had the opportunity to observe other people going through similar experiences.

Case Study: Diana

When I was younger I had an anger problem. I got really mad and I would even break things. Then when I was about 15 I started watching other people get mad and I realized that was what I was doing. Seeing other people get mad helped me to learn to deal with my anger because I watched the things that triggered them. Now when I get mad I usually just tell people that is how I feel and take space for myself until I cool down.

Jean on the other hand experiences limited emotions and has a hard time recognizing them when they occur. She is only able to recognize the effects of her anxiety once she has become so overwhelmed that she has shut down.

Case Study: Jean

I don't really get what feelings are and I don't feel things like love the way you do. It just doesn't go anywhere in my brain. I do shut down when I am anxious or overwhelmed but I don't notice I am that way until it is too late and my brain has already shut down.

Glen explains how depression affects his ability to function and how he experiences emotions with less intensity that most people.

Case Study: Glen

My Asperger's brain is probably predisposed to depression. It seems a lot of us are inclined to these morose states and I for one have been depressed off an on since I was a teenager.

Incidentally, adolescence was when I started to realize I was different. Up until then I had lived with the delusion that something was wrong with all the other kids. I am much more comfortable in the realm of logic and idea than that of emotion so depression has created a bit of a quandary as I am forced to either deal with my emotional state or choose to remain in a dark abyss. For me depression is a lack of my usual exuberant interests such as the virtually extinct nocturnal parrot known as the Kakapo, and the urge to sleep and avoid people more than usual.

Depression aside, as far as I can determine I do not experience emotions to the intensity that other people do. This should not be construed to mean that I do not "care" about people. I do not want people to suffer and I do not want to participate in any activity that would knowingly or unknowingly cause harm to another sentient being. But if I have known you as my friend and neighbor for ten years and you move away, I am not going to feel a sense of "missing" because of this absence.

<u>Acute Empathy:</u>

The official definition of autism describes a lack of empathy or a lack of ability to put ourselves in someone else's shoes or feel what they are feeling as a "social deficit" and most people would probably agree with this description because it has to do with the ability to relate socially to other people. However, many people with hypersensitivity consider empathy to be at least in part, a sensory characteristic.

Contrary to popular opinion, many autistic people do have empathy for others. While having and/or showing a lack of empathy is one of the possible characteristics of autism it is feasible to meet the official criteria for autism and have empathy too. As a matter of fact, some us us actually feel empathy so deeply that when an animal or a person suffers we may experience sensations of physical pain in our bodies.

> **Myth:**
> Autistic people cannot experience
> empathy and caring for others.

Having empathy and showing empathy are two different aspects of identifying with how other people feel. In other words, a person can lack the words to communicate that they relate to another person's experience.

Jeff recalls slamming someone's finger in a door when he was a child and not realizing that he had hurt them. He was unable at that stage of his life to experience feelings of empathy because he did not make a connection between his actions and how other people could be impacted. Now as an adult he is very aware of how other people feel and how his actions affect others. He expresses the desire to help his friends and family when they are in emotional pain albeit in not so conventional ways.

Case Study: Jeff

The day my friend decided her dog was suffering too much in old age I drove her to the vet to have him put to sleep. She told me she was going to miss him so much that she wished she could just hold onto his fur forever. My immediate reaction was to try and think of a way that I could take her dead dog's tail and give it to her. But after I thought about it for a minute I realized that wasn't a good idea. She was just expressing her sadness and I did not need to literally help her hold onto his fur.

I don't think I read faces very well. But I can pick up on other people's emotions in some other way. I started to realize that I could predict when certain people were going to instigate a fight twenty or thirty minutes before they did it when I turned 15.

I also started to pick up on when other people are feeling anxiety before they saw it in themselves. I don't think I am the only one who does this because I mentored a teenage boy with autism and he was non-verbal but I knew that he could tell when I was nervous and when I wasn't. He didn't have to say anything for me to know. He just acted differently towards me.

Diana's story is not unusual. Many people on the spectrum report having extreme feelings of empathy and being so sensitive that it can actually be an impediment. Darla describes what it is like to have a deep sense of empathy.

Case Study: Darla

I am ultra sensitive to other people's feelings, so much so that when I am around someone who is sad or upset I become sad or upset too. I can not watch people suffer without it affecting me very profoundly. Even when something bad happens on the news like a war or fire or animal cruelty, I can't help but be affected physically. The way I typically deal with it is to shut down and go into hiding. I suspect that this type of shut down response is one of the reason that the experts decided that people who have autism can't be empathetic.

The Under & Over Paradox

One of the reasons sensory difficulties can be so difficult to identify is that it is possible to experience over and under-sensitivity at the same time.

Fact
It is possible to have both hyper and
hyposensitivity.

We may be hypersensitive to certain sounds such as a DVD rotating in a player or the snap of a Tupperware lid, but not even flinch at the sound of a firecracker exploding.

Case Study: John's Story

When I was in third grade I fell off the brick wall next to the north side of the building at recess. That afternoon when I got home my mom took me to the doctor because my left arm bone was bent at a twenty-five degree angle and I think you know, that is not supposed to do that. My mom called the school and wanted to know why the teacher had not notified her that I had broken my left arm.

Mrs. Jones said that I hadn't given her an indication that anything was wrong. That is a true statement. I did not feel a thing. I fell off the wall and just kept playing. Well, I've always been this way and this has gotten me into a lot of trouble throughout the years. For example, a few years back, I got my first DVD player for Christmas and when I turned it on, the noise was intolerable to me. It was like a pick ax to my ears. Some certain individuals said that the DVD player shouldn't bother me if I don't even feel the pain of a broken arm and that really made me mad because the sound of that DVD player was painful and those certain individuals didn't believe me.

As we get older and begin to understand the world a little more, we may realize that some behaviors are not considered socially acceptable and make special efforts to keep these behaviors out of sight in certain environments or around certain people.

Myth

People who "self stim" (for example: rock back and forth, flick their fingers in front of their eyes, twitch their necks to the side, flap their hands have no control over when and where they exhibit these behaviors and if they demonstrate control over these behaviors then they can not be autistic.

Fact

Many of us can learn to control when and where we stim.

Case Study: Jane

When I was five, I ran around in circles, flapped my hands, pinned myself between the couch and the wall, flipped light switches off and on and watched sand pour between my fingers for hours on end. Those things were predictable and felt safe to me and at that time, my brain wasn't able to tell my body where I ended and the rest of the world began so I needed predictability somehow.

In middle school I learned to stop flapping my hands and just rubbed my fingers together instead and in high school I learned to put my hands in my pockets whenever I felt the urge to rub or flap. Now I can usually save my self-stims for when I get home and my cat doesn't mind. I've always had an affinity for animals. There is always too much information to process with humans and animals are predictable, easier to understand.

> **Myth**
> Autistic people "self stim" to
> annoy or upset other people.

When Diana was eleven our friend Robert came to visit. I mentioned that we were getting ready to have her evaluated for autism and that in looking over old family videos I realized that she used to flap her hands.

"Used to?" He asked. "She still does. Do you remember the day I stopped by and you were in the middle of reading *Harry Potter and the Sorcerer's Stone* to her brother? She was upset with you because she didn't want me to listen to the middle of the story when I hadn't read the beginning first. In her mind I had to start at the beginning or not listen at all."

I had never thought of what Diana did as "hand flapping" because she always stood so close to me when she flapped that she would automatically hit my arm in the process. I had interpreted this action as "hitting me" not "flapping".

But Robert was right. Diana was and still is definitely a hand flapper. I just never realized it because I had wrongly assumed Diana was trying to hit me. Diana just shook her head and said "How could you not know mom?"

> **Fact**
> Autistic people typically "self stim" to
> relieve anxiety or because it feels good.

Self stimming rarely has anything to do with trying to offend or bother anyone. Today, if you ask Diana about it she smiles and says "flapping my hands makes me happy!"

Tip
If someone you care about pinches, hits, squeezes, bumps into, pulls or pushes other people, this may be a sensory seeking behavior and not an attempt to be aggressive. Instead of punishing, treat the underlying sensory behavior.

Case Study: Andrew

I don't feel an urge to rock at school because it is safe and predictable but I am anxious at the grocery store when too many people are around and grandma's house smells like canned spam.

Rocking helps me cope with the anxiety I feel in a crowd or when the odor of canned spam is lurking about. For those of you out there who think autistics don't have a sense of humor, this is your cue to chuckle.

Mike writes about the role the video game World of Warcraft plays in his life to help him cope with his heightened sensitivity to sound and sight. He is able to focus on the rhythmic patterns of his game and tune out stimuli in his environment that feel overwhelming and painful.

Case Study: Mike:

WoW which was created in 2004 by Blizzard Entertainment is my domain. Currently I am a level 80 and spend most of my waking hours playing. I find WoW to be safer and more predictable than going to school. I can relax when I play and feel a sense of mastery I could only imagine otherwise out there in the jungle of the real world.

It may be possible to withstand certain sounds or lights while in public places such as school or work. But this requires so much energy and effort on our part to "hold it together" during this time that when we get home we "shut down". During this time we may experience a heightened sense of pain or discomfort to noises, touch, smells and or sights. It is as if we have used up all the hot water and need to wait for the tank to heat up the next 20 gallons. An increase in rocking, hand flapping and other sensory behaviors may occur during these times as a way to relieve tension that has built up.

Myth
People's sensory experiences remain constant regardless of time, location and circumstance. If we tolerate something at work or school, we should also be able to tolerate it at home or if we tolerated it last week, we should be able to tolerate it today.

Fact
Our tolerance of sensory stimuli can vary greatly from one circumstance to another.

Sensory input can be more difficult to tolerate during times of transition or change. For example: when job responsibilities change, a new car or home is purchased, death or birth of a family member, a new supervisor or teacher is introduced.

Some of us have trouble experiencing more than one sensation at a time. For example, the feeling of water in the shower may be tolerable in the dark, but overwhelming if the lights are on. Or eye contact may be relatively comfortable to achieve unless there is also background noise from other people talking.

Anxiety

Anxiety is excessive worry and distress over regular life events or events that are unlikely to happen. Thoughts of what might happen dominate the person's day and interfere with their ability to enjoy life and accomplish daily tasks. Furthermore, individuals who have anxiety often report physical sensations such as tense muscles, racing heart, difficulty breathing, sweating, stomachaches, headaches, loss of appetite and trouble sleeping.

If you haven't experienced anxiety for yourself, believe us when we say, it can paralyze! Unfortunately, stimulant medications used for ADHD can actually intensify anxiety[6] and cause an increase in sensory seeking behaviors.

Myth
Inattention and hyperactivity in autistic people are best treated with Attention Deficit Hyperactivity (ADHD) medication.

Fact
Anxiety can often mimic symptoms of ADHD.
Treat anxiety first.

Case Study: Byron

The doctor first prescribed Ritalin to my son Byron when he was 13. He had started having difficulty paying attention in classes and we hoped the medicine would help him focus. He got more irritable and less engaged socially instead. It was very noticeable. I'm talking about decreased communication and eye contact.

Then the doctor consulted with an autism specialist who recommended a low dose of anti-anxiety medication instead. The result was overnight and drastic. Byron got therapy to deal with anxiety in addition to the medication and his problems focusing in school improved.

---

6 http://forums.webmd.com/3/add-and-adhd-exchange/forum/792/3

In order to live comfortably and reach our potential, it is absolutely crucial that any issues of anxiety be addressed. Unfortunately anxiety is frequently overlooked or we are misdiagnosed with Attention Deficit Hyperactivity Disorder (ADHD) or Obsessive Compulsive Disorder (OCD).

Myth
If a person exhibits tendencies such as lining things up, having a specific routine or rituals like turning around before entering a room or washing hands, they must have obsessive-compulsive disorder (OCD).

Fact:
Some people who meet criteria for autism are misdiagnosed with OCD.

OCD is an anxiety disorder in which the person has ongoing, seemingly uncontrollable thoughts and participates in repetitive behaviors to reduce the feeling of discomfort that occurs as a result of these thoughts.

Since people on the spectrum also have racing thoughts and repetitive behaviors, it can be difficult to tell the difference. This misdiagnoses can occur especially if we have less noticeable communication and socialization challenges or if we are used to hiding them.

Unfortunately, autistic individuals who receive a diagnosis of OCD often do not get needed help with communication and socialization. This is why the distinction between OCD and autism is so important. Furthermore, even though OCD is an anxiety disorder, treatment sometimes focuses on eliminating sensory seeking behaviors rather than addressing the underlying anxiety that may be the cause this behavior in the first place.

Teachers used to think that the student who doodled during class wasn't paying attention but doodling or fiddling with your hands can actually improve concentration. Wiggle balls, squishy balls, hats and other sensory tools help some students be successful in the same way that a wheelchair improves mobility and hearing aids improve listening skills for some individuals. In the same way that a student would not be denied a wheel chair, students on the spectrum should not be denied these sensory supports.

> **Myth**
> It is not fair to let some students have wiggle seats, squishy balls, hats or other sensory devises because not all students are allowed to have them.

> **Fact**
> Sensory devises are not toys. They are necessary accommodations.

Many autistic individuals experience extreme intestinal discomfort or even pain and sensory behaviors may actually be an attempt to alleviate this sensation. Studies have shown that when GI issues are properly treated, sensory behaviors like hitting the chest, leaning over furniture and crying often decrease or disappear completely[7].

Some individuals are unable to sense the need to use the bathroom and this can result in loss of both bladder and bowel control. This is one of the reasons it can take a long time for autistic children to become toilet trained.

---

7 Gastrointestinal Issues in Autism Spectrum Disorder Elaine Y. Hsiao, PhD Volume 22 • Number 2 • March/April 2014 Harvard Review of Psychiatry

Their bodies don't necessarily send them the message that they need to use the toilette. In some instances, wetting actually feels comforting and relieves anxiety. Seizures may also impact bladder control. Both anxiety and seizures should be ruled out if bladder control is an issue.

Other Reasons for Anxiety

Problems with sensory integration can be a major cause of anxiety but it is not the only reason. Anxiety can also be a result of:

- ✓ not understanding
- ✓ not knowing what to expect
- ✓ previous traumatic, embarrassing or painful experiences
- ✓ fear of losing something

The important thing to understand is that no one who is in a frightened state for any reason is in a good position to learn, communicate or socialize and people on the spectrum are usually in a state of anxiety that goes unrecognized and therefore untreated.

Exercise #7:

The following Sensory Tool was developed by individuals on the spectrum to help you assess the impact that sensory issues have in your life or for someone you care about. The more checks (or items you respond "yes" to), the greater number of sensory issues the person may have. While this is not a diagnostic tool, it can help identify areas that need modification or adjustment to make life more comfortable. You can answer the questions all at once or take a break in between sections.

The Sensory Tool

Put a check next to each item that is uncomfortable, distracting, irritating or painful to you:

- Difficulty processing more than one sensation at a time
- Skin that itches or hurts for no KNOWN reason
- Limited awareness of body in space
- Limited balance
- Aching joints
- Seizures (any kind)

  Can cause

  - Visual disturbances
  - Tactile disturbances
  - Auditory disturbances
  - Confusion
  - Loss of short-term memory
  - Headache
  - Aggression
  - Other _____

- Gastro-intestinal Issues:
  - Severe cramping
  - Not feeling the need to use the bathroom
  - Fearing loss of body parts
  - Other_____

Sights

Put a check next to each item that is uncomfortable, distracting, irritating or painful to you and circle the specific item(s):

- Faces (especially the eyes)
- Lights
- Bright colors or patterns
- Pictures or decorations on the walls
- Flashing internet adds or television screens
- Christmas lights
- Pages of books
- Small details like specs of dust, scratches, chips or nicks
- Things that are crooked or out of order
- Clutter
- Quickly moving objects
- Crowds of people
- Other_____

Sounds

Put a check next to each item that is uncomfortable, distracting, irritating or painful to you and circle the specific item(s):

- Fabric
- Paper
- Fans, air conditioners, heaters, refrigerators, washing machines, dishwashers, dryers, DVD players
- Pencils, pens, chalk
- Vacuum cleaners, disposals, coffee grinders, blenders, microwaves
- Doorbells, fire alarms, telephones, pagers, buzzers
- Silverware, chip bags, plastic seals
- Cafeterias, gymnasiums, malls, churches, movie theaters, shopping centers, stores
- Dogs, crickets, birds, breathing, coins
- Other _____

Touch

Put a check next to each item that is uncomfortable, distracting, irritating or painful to you and circle the specific item(s):

- Clothing
    - Textures
    - Tags
    - Seams
    - Tightness
    - Looseness
    - Edges
    - Shoes
    - Other _____

- Other people
    - Hugs
    - Pats
    - Squeezes
    - Rubbing
    - Standing next to someone
    - Haircuts
    - Nail clipping
    - Holding hands
    - Kissing and other intimate touch
    - Touch that is unexpected or from behind
    - Other_____

Touch Continued

Put a check next to each item that is uncomfortable, distracting, irritating or painful to you and circle the specific item(s):

- The environment
    - Cold
    - Heat
    - Tight spaces
    - Too much space
    - Sticky
    - Slimy
    - Course
    - Prickly
    - Grass
    - Sand
    - Dirt
    - Other _____

Smell

Put a check next to each item that is uncomfortable, distracting, irritating or painful to you and circle the specific item(s):

- Detergent
- Perfume
- Smoke
- Shampoo
- Makeup
- Hairspray
- Deodorant
- Pets
- Sweat
- Foods
- Fumes
- Paints
- Markers
- Medicine
- Other_____

Taste

Put a check next to each item that is uncomfortable, distracting, irritating or painful to you and circle the specific item(s):

- Spicy
- Sour
- Textures
  - Crunchy
  - Slimy
  - Pasty
  - Mixed
- Fear of swallowing or choking
- Other_____

Common Sensory Behaviors

Put a check next to each category and circle each behavior that you engage in.

- Spinning in circles
- Head banging
- Rocking
- Pacing
- Flipping light switches
- Flapping hands
- Flicking or posturing fingers
- Grabbing crotch
- Compulsive masturbation
- Watching water, leaves, rocks or other items fall
- Tics such as facial twitches, head movements, eye blinking, lip smacking
- Watching fans or other spinning things
- Dropping things
- Flicking doll eyes, levers or flaps
- Spinning parts of toys

Common Sensory Behaviors

Put a check next to each category and circle each behavior that you engage in.

- ▰ Lining up possessions (specify) _____
- ▰ Taking things apart (specify) _____
- ▰ Focusing on one part of an item (specify)_____
- ▰ Repeatedly opening and closing doors, boxes or levers
- ▰ Pinning self in between furniture
- ▰ Wrapping up tightly in blankets
- ▰ Wearing belts or tight clothes
- ▰ Carrying around or filling pockets, bags or backpacks with heavy items
- ▰ Pulling on people or things
- ▰ Head butting or banging
- ▰ Pinching other people's arms or breasts
- ▰ Digging elbow, chin or knee into other people's bodies
- ▰ Picking skin
- ▰ Pulling on faces, ears or hair (self or others)
- ▰ Staring at patterns such as polk-a-dots or stripes
- ▰ Toe walking

Common Sensory Behaviors

Put a check next to each category and circle each behavior that you engage in.

- Avoiding eye contact
- Staring too much at people
- Playing the same game repeatedly
- Singing or saying the same thing repeatedly
- Repeatedly calling others on the phone
- Avoiding physical contact by standing at a distance
- Wandering away or isolating
- Avoiding other sensory input by standing off to the side, staying in own room, avoiding public places
- Watching movie, commercial or TV program scenes repeatedly
- Reading the same book, magazine, list or web page repeatedly
- Refusing to try or eat different foods or foods that touch each other on the plate
- Adjusting items placed by other people
- Other_____

Putting it All Into Perspective

Sensory challenges and anxiety are real and they can affect every aspect of life including the ability to:

- ✓ learn
- ✓ communicate
- ✓ socialize

To reach our full potential in therapy, school and ultimately life our sensory issues and anxiety must be addressed first. Sometimes difficulties in communication and socialization will diminish or disappear entirely once these needs are met.

Each of us interprets the same sensory data differently depending how sensitive we are to any given input which can come through taste, touch, sight, smell, sound, as well as vestibular and prioproceptive sensations. These include balance, awareness of space and body position in addition to awareness of what our body parts are doing in relation to the environment.

Emotions can play a significant role in how the physical body feels. Recognizing and understanding these emotions in ourselves and others along with the ability to talk about these feelings are skills that vary widely from one person to the next. Autistic people may feel some or all emotions to a greater or lesser degree than most people and sometimes we just feel them differently.

Autistic people can and do have empathy. The ways that we demonstrate this understanding however may be unusual. Sometimes our sense of empathy is so intense that we are affected physically.

It is possible to be over-sensitive to some sensory feedback yet under-sensitive to other types of stimuli. Some of us are able to regulate our self stimming in some environments. These stimming behaviors are not done for the purpose of annoying or upsetting other people. They relieve anxiety and feel good. Students with sensory challenges should be allowed to utilize wiggle seats, squishy balls, hats or other sensory regulating devises as necessary accommodations.

Gastrointestinal issues present a major concern for many people on the spectrum and when properly treated can decrease pain, irritability and anxiety as well as associated behaviors.

Other reasons for anxiety include not understanding or knowing what to expect, traumatic and painful past experiences and fear of loss. No one in a state of anxiety is in a position to learn or communicate effectively.

Many autistic people are misdiagnosed with Attention Deficit Disorder or Obsessive-Compulsive Disorder and take medications that can actually increase anxiety. In addition, misdiagnoses can lead to social and communication challenges remaining unidentified.

Sensory experiences can change over time. One day in her sophomore year of high school Diana surprised everyone when out of the blue she put the Boggle game on the table and said "Let's play." Something had shifted. The noise no longer hurt her ears.

Once her body matured and her sensory issues had been addressed, she had no trouble participating with the family in the social and intellectual aspects of game playing. What is especially remarkable is this: Diana had previously been tested by the school and the results had come out with her functioning at a fairly low level. But once her sensory needs were met we quickly discovered that Diana actually has some exceptional spacial, mathematical and language skills. And now when we play Boggle she is capable of finding 5 and 6 letter words in a puzzle that the rest of us overlook.

I often wonder how many children like Diana have marvelous talents, skills and abilities that are masked by intense feelings of anxiety and sensory overload. Sixty years ago these children would have been placed in institutions and forgotten but today you have the opportunity create an environment that lets these skills shine through.

_____Exercise #6: Walk In My Shoes *(pg 67)*

_____Exercise #7: The Sensory Tool *(pg 84)*

Key # 4
Learn My Language

When Diana was thirteen she watched the movie "Blades of Glory" at a friend's house and her favorite thing to say for several months after was: "Nobody knows what it means. It's provocative. It gets the people going!" She said it in the car. She said it at the dinner table. She said it when people came over to visit. She said it to her brother. She said it to me. She said it to her grandmother. I think her grandmother was slightly horrified. I wasn't horrified but I certainly wasn't amused enough to want to hear it for what seemed like the hundredth time.

"It's funny" she said. I asked her why. "I don't know. I just like the way it sounds."

And then she said it again as if that would prove her point.

In high school Diana spent so much time quoting *Napoleon Dynamite, The Princess Bride* and *Harry Potter* that we finally decided to turn it into a family game. The person with the best rendition would be the winner. Diana was usually our undisputed champion and what had once been a daily nuisance became one of our favorite family pastimes.

The implications of repeating the same line over and over again go much deeper than fun and entertainment for Diana. By the time she had graduated from high school she had read the entire *Harry Potter* series, all 4100 pages, 9 times. She came to me one day when she was a sophomore and said "I know what loyalty to your friends is now." You do?" I asked.

"Yes, I learned what it means in *Harry Potter*. I kept reading the passage where Professor Dumbledore talks to Harry about his friends then Ron comes back after he leaves and that is why I got it. Loyalty to your friends is when you stay with them or come back to them even when they have problems."

In other words, Diana relies on repeatedly reading the same passage to help her understand abstract and difficult concepts the same way a small child watches the same Sesame Street or Blue's Clues episode over and over again to absorb new ideas. The brain is hardwired this way to facilitate learning because it knows that repetition will help make the concepts stick.

By the time Diana was nineteen she began to develop the ability to talk readily about some abstract concepts and what she shared with me at that point was completely unexpected. Diana had always longed to be connected and understood the concept intellectually but had never experienced the feeling in her life. She explained that in part, no one had known how to relate to her or help her feel trusting enough to connect.

In the absence of connection she had experienced isolation, mistrust and loneliness instead and I had unknowingly played a part in her feeling this alienation. All the speech therapy, visual supports, patience dealing with meltdowns and listening to scripts for hours on end couldn't fix the isolation that Diana felt.

But what exactly had I done to miss the mark and leave Diana feeling so disconnected in the first place? I had mistranslated. Language is the barometer that lets us know how we are doing and I had completely misread her signals. Diana turned down most invitations to participate in family activities and on the rare occasion that she actually did join us it was short lived. Five or ten minutes in she would say she was bored and ask to go home.

I had assumed that because Diana seemed distant and aloof, that she wanted to be distant and aloof. My interactions reflected this misunderstanding as I made no effort to help her feel more connected.

When Diana's great grandmother was a little girl, communication was simple: She had two ways to talk with people, by writing letters or face to face. If the person she wanted to talk to wasn't in hearing distance she could walk or ride a horse to get to them. Those were her options. Today people need to know how to communicate through:

- ✔ Face to face interactions
- ✔ Talking on the phone
- ✔ Conference calls
- ✔ Talking in small groups
- ✔ Public speaking
- ✔ Social network platforms
- ✔ E-mail
- ✔ Drive thru's
- ✔ Writing letters and notes
- ✔ Typing reports
- ✔ Texting
- ✔ Chatting
- ✔ Video conferencing

Each of these specific types of communication has its own rules and expectations that must be learned and followed in order for understanding between two or more people to occur. We rely on language to:

✔ Make requests

✔ Share experiences

✔ Indicate more information is needed

✔ Solve problems

✔ Communicate feelings, thoughts, preferences, dislikes, boundaries and needs

This presents special challenges because autistic minds are hardwired to process information differently and processing language differently means that we have to work extra hard. We are speaking in a foreign language every single day of our lives.

To put it another way, people on the spectrum are like custom computers living in a Mac and PC dominated world. The code, or programming that society uses for a "PC or Mac brain" will work just fine for the majority of people to ensure desirable behaviors and successful communication occur. But this code is not a match for the autistic brain. We are bound to have a few glitches in the best case scenario and completely crash in the worst if you try to use a program that is not customized for the way our unique brains work.

If you are frustrated because your words seem to fall on deaf ears when you are talking with someone who is autistic, this chapter will give some modifications that you can make to your existing "code" to improve your communication and make sure your barometer is more accurate than mine was with Diana.

The following descriptions explain some of the most common characteristics of autistic communication. Keep in mind that each of us is unique and while these are general guidelines, they may not all fit all of us all of the time.

Sensory Based Language

Neurotypicals (people who are not autistic usually focus communication on the meaning of the words stated and the body language that accompanies these words. We may rely much more extensively on some or all of our senses to understand and relate to the world: Our language may incorporate fewer words and more images, smells, textures, sounds, tastes and movements than what you are used to. We may "do something" instead of "say something". On the other hand, there are those of us who possess exceptional verbal skills.

The traditional solution for our communication delays and differences has been speech therapy which can be very helpful when done well. But entertain for a moment, the idea that our communication differences could actually be beneficial to us if harnessed in the right way. And what if, just what if incorporating some of these differences in your own life actually could improve *your* ability to communicate and accomplish your goals? Autism advocate Temple Grandin often speaks of "the autism gene" as the "gene that gets things done."

Jean Houston in her research in *The Human Potential Movement* discovered that highly creative people are able to accomplish their goals in large part because they are in touch with their senses.

But don't take our word for it. As you read through the following communication differences, try the exercises and see for yourself how crossing over this bridge to our world could improve your interactions with someone on the spectrum and enhance your own ability to accomplish tasks and understand the world.

Visually Based Thinking and Talking

Instead of having words or thoughts pop into our minds, some of us have pictures or images flash through the brain. For example, the term "thinking in pictures" might be literally translated in the brain of an autistic person as someone literally thinking inside a picture. Because some of us are largely visual thinkers we may have dozens or hundreds of these images entering our brains throughout the day. Sometimes these pictures are related to the current topic and sometimes they pop up later at seemingly unrelated times.

Jean describes how images pop into her head in apparently random fashion.

Case Study: Jean

Two weeks ago I went to a new doctor to help me with my leg pains. He asked me if I had ever been treated in the past for this problem. At the time his words didn't go anywhere for me so I didn't say anything except that I couldn't remember. But then this morning I woke up at two o'clock and I was just laying there and suddenly out of no where, the exact image of my last doctor's treatment summary for the pain in my leg popped into my head. I could see it exactly as it was in a box full of other papers that I sorted through over a month ago. So I went to the box and sure enough it was there exactly as I saw it in my head.

Jean is a largely visual thinker and she often struggles to comprehend communication that relies so heavily on words. It may take several minutes or even several days, weeks or months for certain ideas to be translated into a format she can understand. As soon as Jean's brain had translated the doctor's request to fnd out if she had received prior treatment, she was able to recall the necessary information. In this case it took two whole weeks for this understanding to occur.

Visual acuity can be a great advantage. It can assist with test taking and other memory based tasks for those of us with a photographic memory and it can be the basis for creative inspiration if properly harnessed as in the case of many artists, architects and engineers.

But it can also increase nightmares, anxiety and obsessive thoughts when we are exposed to disturbing images. We may not be able to shake those holocaust or horror flick scenes from our memory that other people readily forget. Diana has always has a fascination with horror movies and how they are made. She is able to compartmentalize these images as "not real" in her mind. On the other hand Byron and Jane who discussed their sensory issues in chapter 3 both have repeated and intensely violent dreams any time they are exposed to images of violence.

Visual Supports are for Grown Ups Too

Visual supports are NOT just for children. Writing things down for us instead of expecting that we already understand can help tremendously. Calendars, sticky notes, memos and to- do lists can all be helpful. And discussing information in the same environment that you are talking about can help get your point across clearly.

The need for us to translate abstract words into images or ideas that we can understand may take significantly more time than most people are willing to give when conversing. But this is a critical aspect of the language of autism. It simply takes more time in large part because it is a translation. Here is an example of how Diana has framed the complex idea of having expectations of people into a visual image that makes sense for her:

Case Study: Diana

I don't put expectations on people. They come to me as a blank sheet of paper and write their own expectations on that paper based on their actions. People can erase those expectations and write new ones for themselves. So if you are always late but suddenly start showing up on time, you erase "being late" from the paper and write "on time" instead. This helps me to avoid anxiety and disappointment because I don't expect people to do things.

Visual Language Techniques

1. Anticipate how to translate your words into pictures whenever possible.
2. Provide visual descriptions and supports whenever possible.
3. Ask how we see things.
4. Recognize if and when certain images could be traumatic to us and avoid accidentally exposing us to them.

Sound Based Language

Sometimes we say things because we like the way they sound. We are enjoying the inherent quality of the words themselves. They may have a soothing effect, sound amusing or pleasing in some way.

Most people expect spoken language to have symbolic meaning for ideas or objects. "Duck" represents, a winged animal with a rounded bill that can swim on water and says "quack, quack."

Think of how music and poetry are mediums of communication that can sooth or entertain the listener. For the autistic person, certain words like "duck" can have the same effect as a poem or a song.

Exercise #8: Try out Echolalia for Yourself

Pick a word or phrase that and autistic person you know repeats just because they like the sound of it. Say it out loud 8 or 10 times paying particular attention to how it sounds and how the word(s) feel(s) on your tongue, lips and throat. If you can't think of any words try the following words or sayings:

- ✓ *Digga digga digga digga*
- ✓ *How are you?*
- ✓ *I am fine thank you.*
- ✓ *We want our customers to know we appreciate their loyalty.*
- ✓ *Automaton*
- ✓ *Perpetually*

Quantify for Me

Many of us have a tendency to quantify as much about our worlds as we possibly can to help us understand and communicate our ideas as clearly as possible. While people who are not autistic use terms like "probably", "a great chance", "It's unlikely", "maybe" and "usually" to describe situations, nine times out of ten, an autistic person is going to add a number onto that prediction or statement. Take these real life examples:

- ✓ *I'm a 60% toe walker, 40% heel walker.*

- ✓ *There is an 80% chance I will have to wear a coat tomorrow.*

- ✓ *There is a 75% chance that she will try to set Joe and I up on a date.*

- ✓ *There is a 90% chance I will need to go to the doctor tomorrow.*

Terms such as "probably" are abstract. "There is a 90% chance" is a concrete way to get the same message across.

Tip
Quantify concepts whenever possible instead
of using terms like "probably."
This clarity can help ease anxiety and avoid
misunderstanding.

Comprehension Based Repetition

Thirty years ago therapists and teachers worked to eliminate echoic language. In other words, any time someone repeated a word or phrase over and over again, the therapists tried to stop this behavior. Fortunately, it is now understood that repeating the same thing many times is a helpful and necessary process in the development and understanding of language. If we repeat something, chances are we are trying to understand a difficult idea.

This repetition has often been misinterpreted by people who are not familiar with echoing, sometimes with serious consequences.

Case Study: Joseph

I met Joseph when he was 22. He had been diagnosed with schizophrenia. His mother suspected that perhaps he had been misdiagnosed so she asked me to meet him. His medical records stated:

Patient exhibits delusions of grandeur. Overheard repeatedly stating 'Well, I am king'. Shows signs of hallucinations- Parent reports patient conversing with no one else in the room on numerous occasions.

The psychiatrist had prescribed anti-psychotic medication to deal with these symptoms. When I met Joseph I asked him about his favorite books, movies and television shows. He told me "Monty Python and the Holy Grail" was his favorite movie and he watched it repeatedly.

In "The Holy Grail" King Arthur states "Well, I am King". I asked Joseph why he liked that line in particular. "I really like the way it sounds when King Arthur says it. He is very indignant when he is talking to that peasant and he says *Well, I am king*." Repeating movie lines is a sign of echoic language not psychotic thinking.

I also asked Joseph "Do you ever talk with someone when your mom is not in the room?"

"Yes I do." He responded.

"Who is it?"

"Well, actually, I have an imaginary friend. He basically helps me to make responsible decisions. I talk with him on occasion when I need to behave in an acceptable manner, especially if I will be going out in public and need to be reminded of the proper conventions."

Joseph wasn't hallucinating any more than he was having delusions. He had made up an imaginary friend to help him work through difficult social situations. I confirmed his mother's suspicions that Joseph should be evaluated and he was diagnosed autistic four months later.

Non-verbal Echoing

Communication experts suggest the technique of mirroring or subtly matching the verbal and non-verbal actions of the person you are talking with to demonstrate that you relate to them and their message. It is generally assumed that this is something autistic people are unable to do well because there are many autistic individuals who have a flat affect: Their facial expressions are limited as is their use of gestures.

Mirroring is actually just another way to describe non verbal echoing and many of us have an instinctual ability to echo other people's actions exceptionally well.

It is also not unusual for us to take a special interest in studying verbal and non verbal communication. We often join speech and drama classes or study cultures and anthropology where customs and behaviors can be broken down and systematically learned. So even those of us who are not naturally gifted mimickers can develop exceptional mirroring skills with practice and effort.

Myth
In order to be autistic, a person must have a flat facial expression and limited ability to gesture.

Fact
Some of us do have flat facial expressions and limited or no gestures. Some of us can communicate exceptionally well through body language and some of us may even appear overly dramatic. The ability to mirror others may improve over time and vary from one circumstance and environment to the next.

Case Study: Drew

Drew has always been an actor. He picks up on any behaviors and personalities he is exposed to. When he was very young, four and five, he would imitate the characters he watched on t.v. We all thought it was adorable and hilarious to see a little Bobby Brady or Spider Man running around the house. He imitated them so convincingly. I believe that this is actually the reason he received such a late diagnosis, he was just so good at matching the people in his environment when he was younger. His speech was delayed but that didn't worry me. The doctor said every child talks at their own pace and once he did start talking, it was in complete sentences.

We started to see some fairly significant social challenges when he was a teenager. He thought the other kids were "stupid" and had no trouble telling them. He always had very rigid thinking and this really became a problem in his friendships because he would expect his friends to have the same opinion he did about things or he called them "idiots". I guess this didn't really surprise me because when he was younger he was very controlling when other boys would come over to play. They had to use his legos and light sabers the way he wanted them to or he refused to share his toys.

Scripts & Formal Language

Some of us plug memorized phrases into conversations. They may make sense contextually to other people but sometimes they don't. Oftentimes our ability to memorize is better than our ability to create sentences from scratch. We may rely on this skill to fit a script into a conversation and some of us are so proficient with this technique that it may be difficult for people to recognize that we are not spontaneously using language.

It may sound slightly formal or you might recognize movie, book or song quotes as we frequently include these as responses in conversations. Imagine having a library of quotes in your head and pulling one of these quotes up to respond to what others say instead of creating sentences spontaneously.

That's what many of us do. Take this conversation between George, a popular English professor who specializes in modern literature and his friend Elaine:

Elaine: George! So good to see you. How have you been?

George: Fair to middling. How are you?

Elaine: I'm hanging in there but you know we are still dealing with this crazy property line issue. Would you believe the neighbor came out with his bb gun and was waiving it around like a madman the other day. I told my husband he should call the police.

George: Ah yes! The world is indeed full of peril and in it there are many dark places. But still there is much that is fair.

Elaine: Oh, I know you are right. I shouldn't get all worked up about it. What about your family? How is your son doing these days?

George: Well, I could tell you more about radishes right now than I could about what Jeff is up to. It's been six weeks since we talked but last I heard he was working on a new novel. When he gets into his work we don't see hide nor hair of him.

Unless you too specialize in English literature you might not recognize quotes from Tolkien and Samuel Beckett embedded in his conversation with Elaine. Much of what George says comes from a vast collection of quotes he stores in his brain and plugs in when they seem to fit the conversation. While George relies heavily on idiosyncratic dialogue in face-to-face conversations his writing does not include these scripts. George explains that when he writes, it is easy for him to organize and express his original thoughts.

Because We Are Determined

Often our brains don't give up on an idea. This may be perceived as being stuck and it can help or hinder us depending on the circumstance. When we focus on our careers or parenting it can make us excellent employees and parents but if we get stuck thinking about a bad breakup or whether it's autism or Asperger's, these obsessive thoughts can prevent us from moving on with our lives and being productive.

Case Study: Jane

I have to admit that I have a tendency to get stuck on an idea and this has worked out for me in some instances but it has also created problems for me. I just decided that I was going to be a graphic designer and didn't take no for an answer. I worked through school to pay the bills and got help from the professor in classes when I needed it. If the teacher had an office hour I showed up with my rough draft and worked on it until the teacher said it was acceptable.

On the other hand I sometimes create a scenario in my head of how things are going to turn out and when it doesn't work that way it can put me out of sorts. For example, the other day I had planned to complete a project using a red and blue color scheme. I had figured it out in my heard and when my boss told me that the client wanted different colors I didn't hear her the first time. I went on talking about what I planned to do. My boss had to interrupt me and say "Jane you aren't listening to me and what the client wants." It's not that I don't want to listen when this happens. I do. It's just that my brain has taken off on it's own and I don't hear anything that doesn't fit the direction my mind has gone. I just need to be told when this happens and be given a bit of time to adjust.

Tip

If you see that we are stuck on an idea that is just upsetting us or prevents us from being productive, say "This thought does not help you. Let's talk about what you can do right now to move on."

Quick Dismissal

While we tend to focus diligently on some ideas and tasks, we may
actually do the opposite when faced with new ideas or challenges and give up
before we even try. This is not about being "lazy". There are two main reasons
this happens. First, our brains are hardwired in a way that may not always
allow us to realize there is possibly a solution we just don't see. If we can't see
the solution upfront, then in our minds it doesn't exist.

Second, we often lack the self confidence and belief that we are capable
of handling anything new or difficult and rather than risk the possibility of
trying and being "wrong" it is safer to just avoid the problem in the first
place.

Many years ago, when Dr. Temple Grandin came to South Carolina as the
keynote speaker for the Autism Society Conference she was told by the
hotel clerk that they did not have her reservation. She immediately let the
president of the Autism Society know she could not stay for the conference
because the hotel did not have a room for her. Dr. Grandin was simply
unable to see how she could complete her obligation to speak because of
a scheduling glitch. Someone volunteered their room and the problem was
quickly solved.

A few years later Time Magazine named her as one of the 100 most influential people in the world. We may need help to see how we can go around or over an obstacle because our brains simply may not be able to see possible solutions in given circumstances in spite of our abilities and sometimes even genius in other aspects of life. We may need new tasks broken down into very small and achievable goals.

Tip
Break down new or difficult tasks into
smaller, easy to achieve goals.

Black and White

If you tell most people "I am all ears", there is a 98% chance they will understand that you mean that you are listening carefully to what they have to say. If you tell an autistic person that you are "all ears" there is a 98% chance that they are going to:

1. Be confused because ears make up only a very small part of the human body so it is literally impossible for you to be "ALL ears"

2. Know what you mean because they memorized the definition for this saying but don't really understand why you don't just say "I'm listening"

3. Think you are wrong and have no trouble telling you that you are stupid

When I first met Jean we worked out a plan to help her set a budget. We decided to follow up in two weeks and as I said goodbye , she replied "See you later alligator. I have NO IDEA what that means but I know that's what you people say."

Compartmentalized Thinking

What is interesting about black & white thinking is that we can have areas of our lives where we rely heavily on concrete thoughts and other areas where we may be readily able to see shades of gray. For example, I might be able to understand symbolism in a book or recognize subtleties and flexibility for rules in my professional life but have a hard time understanding that not everyone follows the same rules for behavior and morality that I do in intimate relationships.

This can make it difficult to recognize when someone on the spectrum has areas of black and white thinking. Just because you have noticed abstract thought or flexibility about ideas in one aspect of a person's life does not mean they possess the same level of abstract understanding in other areas of their life.

For example, Damon is a 25 year old man who is very good with computers and logical thinking. He can point out the "rule" that it is inappropriate to speak negatively about a former employer in an interview but when he talks with a prospective employer he forgets not to mention the mistakes his former employer made and brings up complaints during the interview.

Women on the spectrum often recognize how their own relationship rules are not always followed by the people they date. For example, a woman on the spectrum might have the following rules- "always be honest" or "don't cheat on your partner". Even after repeated evidence that a significant other does not follow the same rules, these women may choose to stay in unhealthy or abusive relationships because "I just can't believe someone would- lie (hit me, cheat on me, call me degrading names)."

Case Study: Diana

When Diana was 16 she came home with a boy's class ring. "Do you know what it means when a boy gives you his class ring?"

"Yes." She quickly replied.

"Can you explain it to me?" Based on my own experiences at her age I knew not to assume. When I was 16 a boy had given me his class ring. I promptly put it in my jewelry box until he realized I didn't want to be his girlfriend and he asked me to give it back. I returned it without a second thought, not knowing what to do with it in the first place and only realizing years later how I had unknowingly mishandled the symbolic gesture.

"Well, no. Not really. I don't know what it means." Diana confessed. So I told her "when a boy gives you his ring 9 times out of 10 that means he wants you to be his girlfriend."

The class ring was a symbol that neither Diana or I understood intuitively at age 16. Diana and I needed to be told its meaning in the same manner that a foreign visitor must be taught to replace the American handshake with a respectful bow in Japan or a "bisous" (kiss) in France.

New & Distinctive Every Time

We have a tendency to view each new experience in our lives without relying on similar past experiences. So for example, if we walk down the crowded halls in the mall as children with our parents, we may not generalize the similarities between that experience and the new experience of walking down the crowded hall of our new school or the airport. We may view each new experience as an isolated case and have to relearn the rules in each new setting.

Since the focus is on small details, we may not notice the same things you do or see certain distinctions that are important to you. For example, some of us like Jean may not realize that there is a difference between boys and girls until this distinction is pointed out.

> **Tip**
> Point out similarities and state the rules for us if it looks like we will have trouble generalizing our past experiences to new circumstances.

Focus on the Details

There has been significant discussion about how our extremely heightened sense perceptions may give us a unique ability to focus on minute details that other people may not even know exist. The important thing to remember is that this impacts our communication in a big way both when we listen to what you have to say and when we share our thoughts. We may be trying to listen to you and hearing and seeing all kinds of sights and sounds in the background that we have to filter through in addition to understanding your message.

"Free" Association

Experiences and images relate ideas in the autistic mind. This is a very different process than the neurotypical method in which topics or scenarios relate to each other through largely verbal themes where the person says what they are thinking.

In other words, if you ask a person on the spectrum "What happened today?" The proceeding image of a bird on our morning walk might prompt us to see the following progression of pictures which are related to each other visually but not necessarily related to your question about what happened.

The bird may trigger a memory of the neighbor holding a bird in her hand (notice what we focus on may be a hand instead of the bigger picture). This may remind us of our aunt doing dishes which may then trigger a memory of our sister doing her math homework which might remind us of pencil we stared at in class when we were bored one day.

Before we give you a response, we may have to translate these visual impressions into a verbal description that you can hopefully understand. Some of us are better at this than others, but it takes time and effort regardless of our ability to do so. If we bring up an unrelated topic in response to a conversation, chances are there is a visual relationship in our mind such as the example above that you are not aware of.

In contrast, if the same question is asked to a non-autistic person with strong verbal skills, their response will likely be very close to the thoughts that immediately go through their mind:

> *We walked through the park and saw a bird in the grass*
> *and then we ate lunch at the café across the street.*

Uncensored Honesty- Sometimes

How many times have you avoided telling the truth because you didn't want to hurt someone's feelings or create conflict? Most children learn at a very early age that it's not "polite" to point out when you don't like someone's shirt, hairstyle or the gift they gave you for your birthday. And it is con- sidered to be an insult if you openly observe they are overweight or going bald.

Most autistic people don't view the world this way. We see facts and the observations we make about these facts as neutral. In other words, we don't make a value judgment of "good" or "bad" on the fact that someone is losing their hair or has a dirty house. We just point these observations out the way a scientist would make note of what they observe in an unbiased manner.

So if you give us a gift that we don't like, we are not afraid to say so. If our boss has made a bad decision, we will come out and say it. If someone dies and we are curious about what their skin looks like after rigor mortis has set in, we will ask to see the body. People don't always appreciate this about us. We do our best to accurately state the way things are for the most part, until this gets us into too much trouble.

Case Study: Lindy

I have to admit, I don't have the best filter. I let all my friends and family know that if they have a secret, they CAN'T tell me because I can't keep it. It's like a violent little compulsion that I have to state the facts. It goes something like this: "Have you talked to mom lately? No? Well, I'm not supposed to say anything because she doesn't want people to know yet. . ." At this point I've said too much, I know, but I still can't stop. I confess the whole nine yards in one fell swoop. "She is thinking of putting the old house up for sale and moving in with Aunt Kim."

Case Study: Jill

When I was in second grade, I took it upon myself to let the other kids know: "Santa Clause is not real." At that point I did not understand how the other children could possibly be unhappy with me for stating an obvious fact. But by the time we discussed chapter one of William Faulkner's Absalom, Absalom in college I realized immediately that the other students didn't appreciate my sharing the end of the book before they had the chance to read it for themselves and from that point forward I made it a point to keep my spoilers to myself. It was still several years later before I learned to keep my critical comments about movies to myself so the rest of the audience could enjoy watching. With age and experience I have learned discretion, that just because something is true does not mean it should be stated. In hindsight though, I shudder to think of the trouble I caused those poor nuns who had to deal with a class full of disillusioned students.

> **Myth**
> Autistic people can't lie. Therefore, if someone lies
> they can't be autistic.

At the risk of being too honest, this is a perfect example of the very rigid thinking that some people accuse us of having about the world.

> **Fact**
> There are many times that we will tell you what we think you want to hear because we have learned the hard way that saying what we really think can get us in trouble or may upset people.

Several years ago my colleague Bob asked a client for his opinion about something during his autism evaluation. The man's response was: "Do you want me to tell you what I think you want to hear? Or should I tell you what I am really thinking?" He had learned through the years that people have expectations about what "should" be said in conversations and he made a conscious effort to meet these expectations.

Diana used to tell people, "I have autism".

"No way!" People would often respond with disbelief. "You can't have that. You have good eye contact, you have friends and you are smart."

So Diana adapted how she explained her specific challenges to people by saying "I have sensory problems, I am a bit awkward in social situations and have trouble processing language." Instead of using the word autism, she used the specific criteria that define autism in her case. People responded to her new approach by saying "Yeah, I can really see that about you Diana!"

Both of these examples demonstrate the ability to adapt to our experiences and learn to filter our thoughts before we share them.

Default Response

Some of us have a "default response". A default response is anything we automatically say in reply to something that has been said to us. It may be as simple as "yes" or "no" or "I think so." This default response is not necessarily the answer to your question. We use "default responses" to help us fake it or get by in a conversations that we are having trouble following or feel anxious about. Since we have so many unpredictable and anxiety provoking situations in our lives, this in one way we have learned to deflect some of this complexity so we don't have to deal with it right away.

Case Study: Jean

The other day I had a friend ask me if I would watch her kids for a couple of hours next week. I automatically said yes and then thought about it. I can't take care of her kids. I can't run after them or grab them because of my back injury and I wouldn't know what to say to them if they asked me if they could do something. This happens to me all the time. I just agree to whatever and then realize it's not a good idea. Sometimes people get mad at me for it. It causes problems in my life.

Case Study: Dominic

Dominic called me because he and his son had lost their social security benefits for autism. I had known Dominic and his son for a couple years. Dominic had been unable to maintain a job though he tried diligently. He experienced significant communication challenges. His son was receiving intensive autism supports in a school district that only provided services in the most extreme cases. We often fed them when they came to the office because they had spent what little money they had on gas to get to the office so the ruling came as a surprise to me on all fronts.

I spoke with the social security representative who told me that Dominic and his son were not eligible because he had "lied about having autism". I asked the representative why she came to this conclusion and she explained that Dominic's renewal paperwork did not list "autism" under the question "What is your problem?" He had mentioned a back injury instead. Then during his phone interview she asked him if he had autism and his first response was "no".

I explained to the worker that neglecting to mention autism in the paperwork and saying "no" during the interview were both examples of how Dominic's communication was affected and yes he and his son both did have autism. I helped him revise his paperwork and disability was eventually reinstated for both of them.

Tip
To find out if our "yes", "no", "maybe" or "I think so" is a default response, ask us to re-state in our own words, the intent of the conversation or the request you are making. If we are not able to give a reasonable answer, then chances are we are relying on a default response and you will know for future reference that you should check for comprehension instead of assuming we understand.

Unaware or Hypersensitive to Faces

Just because some of us have a hard time looking at people's faces does not mean that we aren't interested or are just oblivious to you. Eye contact may be especially difficult for us because we can actually be hypersensitive to all of the information that is expressed through the face. Sometimes we are overwhelmed by all of the information that we pick up. Linda describes her experience:

> I have always felt a certain discomfort bordering on pain when I make eye contact with people and I have to resist the urge to contort my face. But I remember even as a young girl that I could focus my attention on the mouth and get a pretty good read on how the person was feeling.

Brad's experience is very different:

> *The realization suddenly occurred to me that I just don't know how to read faces. I get them wrong. Consistently. It explains a lot of awkward blunders I have made throughout my life. I had to literally go through and memorize what muscles do what to mean what specific emotion.*

Notice how Linda has learned to compensate for the discomfort felt when making eye contact and she has developed a system to interpret emotions. Brad on the other hand does not posses the natural ability to read faces and has had to memorize the exact expression paired with the emotion.

A Good Reason

In order for us to really understand and be able to follow through on requests, we may need to have a good reason to do so. If something does not appear logical or as if it is going to directly benefit us then it doesn't make sense for us to spend energy on it. This is one of the reasons many of us have a hard time participating in "small talk". We can't see how it is useful in our lives.

Case Study: Landon

We hired Landon in 2011 to stock and keep track of our inventory. Landon knows exactly what we have and if we are missing one spoon or straw he knows it. This makes him the perfect employee for our back room. Right away we noticed that there were some things I would tell him to do that he just wouldn't do. His job coach figured out that the only time Landon would not follow through was if he didn't have a good explanation, so we started making sure that Landon understood why he was performing a specific task and we haven't had problems since. We just always give directions with a reason why.

Talking to Ourselves

The traditional way to look at communication is as a means for a person to express wants, needs, desires, dislikes, requests, and experiences with other people. But communication also serves the function of helping us to under-stand and cope with life. While anyone can talk to themselves, those of us on the spectrum frequently self-talk by:

- ✓ writing lists (this can be anything from things we need "to do", to ideas we want to understand to things that interest us)
- ✓ having conversations with ourselves in our heads or out loud
- ✓ artwork and doodling
- ✓ carrying symbolic items
- ✓ getting tattoos, piercings or wearing certain clothing

Case Study: Byron

Byron is a list maker. From the time he started writing he would make lists. He especially likes to make lists of the credits for television shows and movies that he likes. He carries a little notebook around with him and writes the credits down over and over again, the same ones. He has a notebook full of Sponge Bob credits and another one with Bionicles in it. Byron also talks to himself constantly just under his breath.

At first these behaviors really worried me because they just stood out as so odd but as he got older I could see how talking with himself and writing these lists helped to calm him and set his mind at ease. Byron would especially talk with himself after he got home from school. He would lock himself in his room and talk for about 20 minutes before he would come out and get started on homework. His therapist said this is his way to wind down after dealing with school all day.

<u>Case Study: Jeff</u>

I started getting tattoos about 3 years ago. My first tattoo was a compass and I asked the guy to put it on my arm upside down so that I could see it. He said most people put it so other people can see it right side up. I told him I was getting it for me to look at not other people. I use that tattoo as a reminder to focus and it worked so well that I got another one and another one.

Each of my tattoos has a meaning and reminds me of something-like not to worry or to ask other people questions. It's become a routine for me now to get a new tattoo. I'll probably grow out of it at some point or have to grow out of it when I run out of space.

> **Tips**
> 1. Give extra time (at least 10 seconds) before expecting a response)
> 2. Eliminate background noises whenever possible
> 3. Write things down for us

<u>Special Processing Issues</u>

Some of us got in trouble often as children and might have been labeled with "Attention Deficit Disorder" or "Oppositional Defiant Disorder". Our parents and teachers may have said "I know he/she can hear me. He/she is just being difficult and choosing not to listen." Or "He/she could do it yesterday. That means he/she should be able to do it today too." What they didn't know is that there are other conditions which can contribute to processing difficulties. Autistics may have one, all or any combination of the following:

> **Central Auditory Processing Disorder.** This means that our ears hear sounds accurately, but our brains scramble the messages so these sounds don't make sense.

High levels of anxiety which make processing language more difficult in some circumstances.

Background noises and other sensory stimuli such as fans, running water, voices, music, dust particles, or fabric patterns, can make it next to impossible to hear someone speaking.

Some kinds of **seizures** can cause a person to miss out on large parts of conversations without the other person even knowing that anything is wrong.

Exercise #10: Seizure Red Flags

✔ Does the person seem to be unable to perform tasks that they have previously learned?
✔ Does the person have staring spells- their eyes glaze over briefly and wander off into the distance?
✔ Does the person frequently seem to forget conversations or events?
✔ Does the person rub the area between their eye brows and complain of headaches or discomfort?
✔ Does the person fall out of their chair or fall down for no known reason?
✔ Does the person rage or get angry for unexplained reasons?
✔ Does the person perform repetitive movements, such as hand rubbing, chewing, swallowing, lip smacking, eye blinking or walking in circles?
✔ Does the person have twitching arms or legs?
✔ Does the person accidentally wet themselves even though they are toilette trained?

Special thanks to Bob Egelson who contributed to this screening.

Language Comparison

Autistic

Neurotypical

Processing time: Can be up to 10 seconds for simple statements and a day or longer for some ideas.

Processing time: Immediately in most cases.

Often appreciate the sound of particular words or expressions regardless of meaning- sensory based.

Focus primarily on meaning.

Don't get tired or bored of repetition. May need multiple repetitions of same phrase and rewording of phrase.

Expect new phrases building on preceding sentences without repetition. Repetition is boring and annoying.

Concrete, literal, black and white.

Abstract, symbolic, shades of gray.

Phrases and concepts do not easily generalize: May see each type or characteristic as distinct and separate.

Easily generalized to new conversations and situations.

Visually based/with free association.

Thought/ word based.

Can mix hearing with other senses: smell, tastes sight, touch.

Primarily auditory and visual.

Completely honest by nature- no filter, from thought straight to words, but may learn to filter.

Strong filter- may withhold information or phrase tactfully to preserve someone's feelings.

Often presents with flat affect but prefers others to have animation so meaning can be more easily interpreted.

Varying degrees of animation depending on individual and circumstances.

Memorize scripts that can be plugged into conversations.

Impromptu language.

May have difficulty interpreting facial expressions, tone of voice and non-verbal cues and rely mostly on literal words.

93% of communication is nonverbal.

Putting it All Into Perspective

Communication makes it possible to share experiences, thoughts, feelings, boundaries and needs, ask for more information, and solve problems. Everyday communication for people on the autism spectrum is often compared to the experience of trying to live and communicate in a foreign country without knowing the language and customs. There are some common distinctions of autistic communication which include:

✔ Sensory based, visually based and sound based language

✔ quantification

✔ repetition for the purpose of comprehension, nonverbal echoing (sometimes referred to as mirroring or imitating)

✔ relying on scripts and/or formal language

We may get stuck on certain ideas and quickly dismiss other concepts without fully exploring them, rely on black and white thinking in some or all cases, have difficulty generalizing experiences rather than grouping similar events or categories together, and focus on small details that other people don't even notice.

Our thoughts may be freely associated together and we may be honest to the point that others may be offended or hurt. We may learn the ability to filter these thoughts as we have more experiences and with maturity.

Some of us may pretend to comprehend more than we really do and say "yes" or "no" as a default response to something we don't understand as a coping mechanism to avoid unwanted attention or stay out of trouble.

We may have difficulty recognizing or paying attention to faces. Some of us are actually hypersensitive to faces. It helps us follow through with expectations when we understand the reason we are doing what we are doing rather than just going through the motions because someone else says that we should.

We may utilize self-talk to help us process and understand information. This can be verbal or in the form of artwork, writing or looking at symbolic items that we carry.

We may have processing issues that make communication especially challenging:

✓ seizures

✓ central auditory processing complications

✓ anxiety

✓ background noises can all affect the ability to speak and understand effectively

I have to admit as a parent, I've been known to make the same blunders I advise other parents to avoid in my role as a professional. Some of these mistakes are minor and some of them like assuming Diana did not want to create connections leaves me with nagging regrets and wondering "what if I had done things differently?"

Fortunately, Diana refers to these parenting errors as "new information" so we move forward together, imperfect but armed with data to help us make different choices for the future. We are working on connection now and Diana is often quick to remind me of her favorite quote, "Never a mistake, always a lesson".

<u>To Do List</u>

_____Exercise #8: Try out Echolalia for Yourself *(pg 106)*

_____Exercise #9: Be More Autistic *(pg 113)*

_____Exercise #10: Seizure Red Flag Screening Tool *(pg 126)*

I want people to like me. And for the first few minutes when I meet someone   new, I feel a brief moment of acceptance. Then I open my mouth and say some-thing wrong. I see it in their faces. They back away and I know they think I am weird. They don't want to be around me.
Anonymous

I've been told just what to do
Where to look and point my view
All the things that I could be
I think I learned in therapy
Am I just a shadow you drew?
Imagine Dragons

Key # 5
Relate to Me &
Create An Authentic Connection

Nathan and I were separated by the glass window that punctuated my freedom and his status as an inmate in the county jail where we met. We spoke to each other through an old fashioned speaker phone that reminded me of my childhood and the seventies.

Nathan's grandmother had asked me to meet with him because he was facing a possible 5 year prison sentence for stealing a car. She hoped he would be willing to disclose his Asperger's and seek treatment in lieu of jail time. "I know my grandson did not commit this crime alone. He refuses to learn to drive because he has so much anxiety over the idea of getting behind a wheel. Nathan is a sponge and he will pick up on whatever behaviors he sees, good or bad. I fear he will leave jail having learned all the wrong things and he will be destined to repeat the behaviors that got him here in the first place".

Nathan admitted to the police that he was a passenger when the car was stolen but he refused to "rat the other guys out". He told me that he didn't want to talk about the incident but he would have a conversation out of respect for his grandmother who had raised him from the time he was three.

He explained that he had been very lonely and was dating a girl "because she was there and available" even though they had nothing in common and he knew she wasn't the best influence. She had introduced Nathan to the other two involved in the theft. "I went along with it but I didn't think about it at the time. I just got in the car with them" he explained. " I feel bad now because it caused a lot of trouble for the lady who owned the car. She was a single mom and all."

I asked him if I could make recommendations to the court for treatment as a sentencing alternative to prison time based on his diagnosis.

He looked me straight in the eye. "Can you guarantee if Asperger's goes on record, when I get out of here in seven days or seven years, nothing negative will happen when people know about it?" It was a rhetorical question and I knew it.

Nathan was willing to keep his Asperger's a secret at the risk of five years behind these bars. He had decided it was better to have the label "felon" attached to his name than the label of "Asperger's".

Nathan's circumstances may have been extreme but his desire to fit in is not. Just as Diana has longed for a connection with others, Nathan wanted to belong. He had hopes and aspirations to support a family some day and he worried that if people knew about his diagnosis it would prevent him from reaching this goal. He cared about what other people would think of him.

Myth
People on the spectrum do not care what other people think.

There is a tendency to assume that autistic people are somehow immune to the human condition, without feeling, conscience or regard for others. This has led to traditional therapies that emphasize socialization or getting people to "behave in an acceptable manner". Because many of our behaviors are considered unusual, irritating, or contrary to social conventions we are often expected from an early age to conform to thoughts and behaviors that are not in line with our natural state of being.

Case Study: Brad

I realized early on that my dad was disappointed in me and that I would never live up to his expectations. He wanted a self assured son who played ball. Not a nervous autistic kid who paced, twitched his head and was interested in lepidoptera (the study of moths and butterflies).

He used to say 'knock that nervous head twitching off and stop chasing those butterflies kid. There's nothing wrong with you". As hard as I would try, I would forget and start twitching again. I joined the baseball team for a while but I just couldn't coordinate my body or follow the rules. so I stood out like a sore thumb on the field. I was ashamed for a long time of who I was and denied the fact that I had autism. The fact is that I like butterflies and I pace and twitch my head when I am around other people. I never hurt anyone and I never broke the law. I make a decent living as a professor. I would have liked for my dad to be ok with that.

Acting "Normal"

Those of us who don't possess an innate ability to mirror other people are quickly identified as a result of our unusual behaviors and trained to act "normal" so we can "fit in" from an early age. In other words either we are taught how to mirror non-autistic behaviors or our natural abilities to mirror, mask our autism and we fake being normal. We are regularly expected to:

- ✓ Have more eye contact
- ✓ Gesture more frequently
- ✓ Talk more frequently
- ✓ Talk about subjects that don't interest us
- ✓ Replace our formal communication style with informal language and slang
- ✓ Stop our instinctual sensory behaviors (e.g. pacing, rocking, flicking)
- ✓ Be in closer proximity to other people and greet them with hugs, handshakes or kisses
- ✓ Talk with people we can not relate to

And while non-autistic people expect us to conform to these norms of society, ironically it is rare to encounter someone who is not autistic who is willing to reciprocate and match or mirror autistic communication styles by doing any of the following:

- ✓ Make less eye contact
- ✓ Talk in depth about our special interests and avoiding small talk
- ✓ Focus on details such as dates, names or trivia
- ✓ Communicate using formal dialogue
- ✓ Rock, pace, or watch leaves or sand fall
- ✓ Keep a wider physical distance

Acting "normal" does not mean we are normal or that we feel normal or even that we understand what normal is. Acting "normal" does allow us to go about our lives without drawing unwanted attention to ourselves for behaviors that can be misinterpreted or misunderstood. In other words, it keeps us out of trouble.

Exercise #11: Social Expectations

Part 1: Take 5 minutes to think about the expectations for "normal" behavior that have been placed on an autistic person you care about and list some of these expectations below (e.g. this list might include things like "the teacher wants a quick response to questions", "I expect a hug", "to attend noisy birthday parties").

_____

_____

_____

_____

_____

Part 2: Take 5 more minutes to think about any ways that you have adapted your communication style to match or mirror this person (e.g. this list might include things like: ask for a hug before giving it, rely on texting instead of phone calls, or repeat a favorite phrase together).

_____

_____

_____

_____

_____

Identity Dilemma

Combine our challenges to understand the social world with pressure to conform to other people's expectations of how to think and behave from an early age and the result is that we don't have a chance to find out who we really are. Steven Paglierani, author, therapist and creator of "The Emergence Theory", describes it like this:

> Imagine if everyday of your life, you had to imitate normal, all the time never really understanding what it is you're trying to do, let alone why it makes you feel so bad. In other words, imagine never being encouraged to find and be yourself. God, what a cruel thing to do to a human being. Ironically, because medical professionals use statistical norms as measures of health, they see getting these folks to imitate normal as the path to health.

Steven is right. Imitating normal does not equal comprehension, health or happiness.

Case Study: Sharon

I'm 46 years old and I honestly have no idea who I am. I know what I DO, What I'm good at and what my faults are, but if you ask me at the core, the essence of who I am, I have absolutely no idea how to answer that question. I recall spending a lot of time when I was younger observing other girls and trying to imitate how they walked, their facial expressions, what they wore and what they said. I didn't realize it at the time that I was just copying other people but in hind-sight I do remember feeling very uncomfortable. I was very awkward and desperately wanted to hide that fact from people.

Even today I feel like I don't know how to be natural in my expressions or posture. I don't really know how to describe it except that my face and body feel contorted but I try very hard to hide this. I was so afraid of getting in trouble that I focused a lot of energy on making other people happy, never having an opinion of my own.

My best friend growing up was diagnosed with Asperger's when he was 9. He had no problem stating his opinion and being his own person. I think this is why I liked being around him so much. Even though we both were on the spectrum he was like my opposite in many ways because he never seemed to worry about what other people thought.

I obsessed about the free spirited heroines in books and movies like Jane Eyre and Jo March. I wished I could be like them, but I am just too worried about what other people will think and since I don't really have a good sense of what is normal, being quiet and going along with other people have been my ways to avoid scrutiny.

Sometimes the feeling of isolation is profound because we have not had the opportunity to relate to other people who are similar to us.

Case Study: Graham

Hi, my name is Graham and I was diagnosed with autism when I was 6 years old. When I turned 16 I thought that I must not be from this planet because I didn't know anyone else who was like me.

I told my therapist and he said it was because I've got autism and I never met anyone else like me before. My therapist said I needed to meet other young people with autism so I wouldn't feel like an alien. So my mom helped me go to a social group for teens and I found out my therapist was right. Other people with autism can feel like an alien too.

Special Considerations

There are some specific issues that may play a significant role in how we perceive ourselves and how we are viewed by others. An awareness of these issues goes a long way in helping you discover who we are. Awareness of some of these issues may also prevent misunderstandings that can cause people we care about to feel hurt or unnecessarily worried.

Dealing with Prejudice

Sometimes social expectations are taken to an extreme. If you think the price Nathan was willing to pay to keep his diagnosis secret seems irrational, consider these people who have chosen to be open about being autistic:

Case Study: Janice

I worked as one of three receptionists at a local dentist office and received raises and excellent employee evaluations every time, until I went for an autism spectrum diagnosis. I told my boss about it and two weeks later after six years of exemplary employment, she cut back my hours and gave them to one of the other receptionists. Then about a month later I got laid off. I can't prove it of course but I had done nothing differently during that time except disclose that I have been diagnosed with autism.

I know people tell me I should fight to get my job back but honestly, I wouldn't even feel safe working for a boss that discriminated against me. It would be like having an anti-Semitic bake the challah for the wedding. Only the baker and Yahweh would know what went into that bread and I for one wouldn't be sure it was exactly kosher.

Case Study: Ben

I am called a "freak" and a "F-ing retard" by the other guys on the job. I don't like it but you get used to it.

Exploitation and Manipulation

Individuals on the spectrum can be especially at risk for for being taken advantage of financially, sexually and at work or school. When Jim was in school the other students recognized there was something different about him and they used this difference as a basis to tease and lure him into trouble.

Case Study: Jim

At school there was a group of boys that knew I was pretty gullible. They would teach me cuss words or insults and tell me to say them to the teacher or other kids. I'm autistic so of course I did what they said and of course I got in trouble. Those were the days when teachers would smack your hand with a ruler for punishment. I also got my tail kicked by the other kids when I would unknowingly insult them. There was one boy in particular who would stab me with a pencil when the teacher wasn't looking and then if I cried out the teacher would punish me so I learned to keep quiet in the classroom no matter what the other boys did. They took it upon themselves as a challenge to see how far they could go with it before I would crack.

Jean has dealt with both sexual and financial exploitation throughout her life.

Case Study: Jean

When I left home I lived in my car for a while and then I met a guy who said I could stay at his house. He wanted sex and I thought that was his right to expect it as payment for living at his place. I didn't get until years later that I could have done something different.

Basically, if someone tells me I need to do something I just do it without thinking about it and then I might realize later it wasn't a good idea. Sometime people will say I should buy something for them and I just say "OK." and then my friends will say I shouldn't do that because I don't have a lot of money.

Online Communities and Video Games

It is not unusual for parents and support professionals to have concern about time spent in on-line communities or on video games and the potential for exploitation. While these concerns are legitimate, on-line communities and video games can actually help us gain skills, knowledge and practice with social interactions in the same way books music and movies can help. They can also help us cope with our anxieties and sensory overload.

Aaron describes how he developed an understanding of the abstract concept of "willpower" by using a specific technique in a video game.

Case Study: Aaron

Here is a non-scientific way of looking at it. In the game, there's a concept built-in called HEAT. It's basically your Tension Gauge, and it allows you to pull off special moves against enemies. HEAT in the video game is comparable to willpower in the physical world and it's using that willpower to achieve. I wish people would achieve with that same HEAT in the real world but non-violently.

Shawn discusses the role online virtual worlds have had in his ability to build relationships and how other people's responses affect his ability to interact with them.

<u>Case Study: Shawn</u>

If I want to work on something like going up to a person I don't know and initiate a conversation with them I work it out in Second Life first with my avatar. There is a misnomer that just because I have autism I don't want to engage with people face to face. I don't hate being around people, I'm just not very good at it and therefore it isn't very comfortable for me or people who don't know me well. Sometimes I initiate an interaction but it isn't always reciprocated probably because the person doesn't know how to respond to my less than graceful approach.

I will admit that there have been times in my life where my computer use has been excessive. Typically when life has been especially stressful I tend to put my focus on-line. I have had to learn balance.

My piece of advice for concerned parents is-- don't try and take away computer use entirely. Instead make sure that your son or daughter feels safe in their physical environment and that they have activities that they enjoy made available to them as alternatives to computer use so they have a choice to do other rewarding activities.

There is one more thing I would like to say. My best friend also loves gaming and we got to be good friends as a result of our common interest and the fact that we were able to talk about real life issues like feeling isolated in the context of our gaming experience.

The internet has created opportunities for friendships and connections with like minded people that did not previously exist. Many autistic people who never experienced the feeling of connection or friendship report that they are now able to have these experiences on-line.

<u>Case Study: Aaron</u>

The internet is a great place to meet people that have something in common with you. I have always felt isolated because I don't have friends that live near me, a problem that being on-line eradicates.

You have to use common sense if you are meeting new people online and follow the same rules you should follow in person. You don't give your real name, address or personal information to anyone until you know you can trust them. But overall, I have met some very good people online including my best friends.

Paranoia

Twenty and thirty years ago, autistic people were often mis-diagnosed with schizophrenia. In part this happened because many autistic behaviors such as echoing and sensory experiences were misinterpreted as hallucinations and delusions.

But there is more to it than that. We often struggle to interpret people's actions and because we don't have a good sense of how to read behaviors or circumstances we feel a great deal of uncertainty over situations and events that most people understand and simply take for granted. We learn that our internal guidance system does not match what other people tell us about how the world should be interpreted and therefore we have difficulty trusting that world. We may often assume the worst.

Case Study: Byron

Just the other day Byron came home and said that his English teacher was mad at him. When I asked Byron why he thought that he told me the teacher had returned everyone else's graded paper and held onto his to "make and example" of him. When I asked Mr. Davis about the incident he explained that he had kept Byron's paper but it was because it was well written and he wanted to use it as a *positive* example for some of the other students who were having trouble.

As we get older this mistrust and fear can extend to work and other aspects of life as we make associations with events or circumstances that would seem unrelated to most people.

<u>Case Study: Jean</u>

I have been Jean's case manager for 7 years now. When she started working for a store several years ago, she was convinced that the supervisor had asked her to sign a paper so she could get access to her bank account and talk to her doctors. When I asked the supervisor about it she said that the papers she had her fill out were a W-2 form and the standard new employee paperwork.

At one point I wanted to get Jean supplemental services but she was not willing to give me the required information and sign the paperwork because she was worried that the government would use it to make management decisions about her seizure medication. After a little digging I discovered that she had read an article on-line about a family that had run into some trouble with their managed care and thought the papers I wanted her to fill out were somehow related to that.

One day Jean had come across a plastic snake on the side of the road where she walks every day. She though that one of the other employees had put it there to scare her because they had talked about snakes the day before.

Jean made an association between the plastic snake and a conversation she had the day before that most people would assume was a coincidence. This does not qualify Jean for a diagnosis of schizophrenia. It is however an example of concrete thinking, the conversational associations we talked about in Key 4 and how the unpredictability in her life has caused her to be hyper vigilant about details that most people take for granted.

<u>Mind Reading</u>

Making assumptions about the plastic snake is an example of how Jean assumes that other people have the same information and perspective that she does. The other employee had no idea where Jean lives let alone where she walks each day though Jean assumed that they did.

We may need to be specifically taught that other people do not necessarily have the same information or perspective that we do about things.

Case Study: Sharon

The old theory of mind test where you see an item moved from one place to another and assume that someone who left the room would know it had been moved too can be misleading. I never failed that test because it was represented on paper which plays to my visual strengths. But that doesn't mean my theory of mind has always been stellar. It took me a long time to realize that other people have different rules about life than I do and I distinctly remember the day my mother said "honey, don't be mad at me because I don't know what you are thinking. People can not read your mind". I was 21 at the time and that was a huge epiphany for me.

Just because a person understands that perspectives may vary in some circumstances does not mean they understand this concept in all aspects of their lives. For example, a person might be able to analyze movies or literature and see the character's different points of view but be unable to do so in their own intimate relationships or regarding their special interest.

Burnout

Because we are dealing with anxiety, as well as sensory and processing challenges, it is common for us to become overwhelmed or burnt-out in circumstances that would not cause problems for most people because our system which regulates how we feel may be delayed or set at a very high threshold.

Burnout can cause us to shut down for several days or several months. We become physically, emotionally and mentally exhausted. During this time we may have a lack of energy or constant fatigue, inability to sleep well, greater degrees of anxiety, depression, and hypersensitivity, forgetfulness, inability to concentrate, poor appetite and frequent illnesses.

Jean explains how she says "yes" to invitations and activities without considering the impact they will have on her health.

Case Study: Jean

My brain does not tell me when to stop. Yesterday after dog sitting for six hours I went to Bible study. Mavis asked me to go out for dinner afterwards. I didn't think to say "no" even though I have a back and knee injury and had been on my feet since four am. I just went along with everybody and didn't think. That is just the way my brain works. I won't realize that I am overwhelmed until I shut down completely and then I won't be able to do anything.

Pacing activities, taking breaks and setting limits can be challenging but what could be a problem in some situations actually works to Shawn's advantage because he has found a career that plays to his unique rhythms and allows him to take breaks when needed.

Case Study: Shawn

In college I burnt out after my second year. I had been taking 18 credits every semester and had to drop out because I started flunking classes. This has been a pattern throughout my life.

Now when I am working on a project for work, I will pretty much focus to the exclusion of all else on that one objective until it is completed. I will work 14 to 16 hours a day without breaks and then when the project is done, I will crash for three or four days. Fortunately, videography is a career where my cycles and late night work hours are tolerated and even rewarded. I could never work a regular 9 to 5 job. It just wouldn't match my natural rhythms and drive to complete things.

Tired, Hungry and Thirsty

Because of our tendency to hyper-focus and the fact that our bodies don't always communicate our needs, we may forget to take breaks, to eat, drink and sleep. This can result in dehydration, blood sugar drops and exhaustion. We may need reminders to take care of our physical needs.

Case Study: Shawn

I can get so engrossed in a project that I am working on that I don't even stop to get a drink or eat anything let alone go to the bathroom. I do realize that I function better when I've taken care of myself but I literally have to be reminded.

Death and Loss

Perhaps one of the most disconcerting misunderstandings for family members is how people on the spectrum often perceive and deal with death. Our responses when someone dies may come across as insensitive and uncaring.

Myth
Autistic people do not feel a senses of loss
and don't care when someone dies.

Fact
Autistic people often view death as a natural and inevitable state of the life cycle rather than a tragedy. Consequently, it is not something to fear or regret but simple a fact to be accepted as a circumstance outside of human control. This does not mean we do not care.

Acceptance of the inevitable life stages including death is a "logical" way to deal with the loss of a family member, friend or pet but acceptance does not mean we do not care.

Case Study: Diana

When my friend Nick died I did not cry until I saw him at the viewing. I was the last person to take his picture and one of the last people to talk to him. As far as I am concerned, he still lives inside of me. He helped me when we were kids to do things that were hard for me. I wanted to have friends and he helped me to achieve that. He would have been 21 this year. Every year on his birthday I take time to remember him.

A Note About Crying

Some of us cry "all the time" when we are very young and then may go through a stage where we don't cry at all. A lack of crying may be a result of not feeling sadness or hurt, but not necessarily. We may feel emotions but simply not have an urge to cry. It is a good idea to check with us on how we are feeling instead of just assuming. We may need help in identifying and coping with our emotions even during circumstances when we do not have the urge to shed tears.

Autistic Parenting

Autistic men and women do have children and can make good, even exceptional parents.

> **Myth**
> Autistic people do not have children.

> **Fact**
> Autistic people can and do have children.
> We may have qualities that are ideal for
> parenting.

Parenting does present a particular set of problems that can be especially challenging for autistic moms and dads: sensory overload from dirty diapers, throw up and crying as well as the fact that children have their own routines can create extreme stressors. Explaining abstract concepts and teaching appropriate behaviors can often be difficult to achieve. Autistic parents respond to these challenges in a variety of ways.

Case Study: Jeff

When my son was diagnosed with autism my mom came with us to the clinic and said I was exactly like him when I was his age. So I decided to get an evaluation for myself and was diagnosed with autism too.

There have been times when my own experiences have helped me know what to do as a parent. For example, my son went through a superhero stage where he wanted to wear different costumes all the time. My wife was very concerned and so was the therapist but I remembered doing the same thing and this is one of the ways I learned about roles and rules. So I helped my son make different costumes and explore the different roles in that manner. He is 16 and has outgrown the desire for costumes but has an obsession with the piano and martial arts. I've made a studio in the garage where he can practice the piano and do his workouts. He has been composing and recording songs since he was 9.

Some parents report that they must learn skills required to care for their children systematically because the instinct may not come naturally.

Case Study: Claire

I didn't have the natural mothering instinct that other mom's seem to possess but I made up for this lack by trying really hard to be a good mom. I was very structured and made sure my children were well fed, safe and met their school responsibilities just like any other parent would. I just didn't feel like it came instinctually to me and I had to make a thoughtful effort.

Case Study: Richard

My husband and our son Ryan are like two peas in a pod. They are so similar that they often have trouble getting along. Richard has always been a good provider but he does not and has never understood how his need to have everything in a particular order has affected Ryan and their relationship.

Jean recognized that she had limited parenting skills and decided to give her baby up for adoption because she felt she would receive better care from an adoptive parent.

Case Study: Jean

I found out I was pregnant and I knew, just knew that I didn't know what to do for a baby. I could hardly take care of myself. So I planned to give the baby up for adoption. I had a family picked out and everything. But my family got really upset and said it wasn't right to give the baby up so I kept her. But I just couldn't handle it and my sister and her husband ended up raising her when they realized it wasn't a good thing.

Gay, Transgender and A-sexual Identities

Because we do not always rely on the same patterns of discrimination and categories that society sets up to define relationships, a large percentage of autistic people do not subscribe to the usual gender roles for ourselves and in relationships. This means we may be gay, bi-sexual, or transgender. Some of us are also a-sexual preferring not to have intimate physical contact at all.

Case Study: Ashley

I don't really feel like I am a girl. I can't really relate to what that means to be a girl. I think maybe I was meant to be a male because I relate so much better to males. This is not something that I can talk about at home because I think my family would not understand how I feel. I think it would bother them to know that I am transgender. At school my friends call me Evan and they don't have a problem with it.

Case Study: Erin

I just don't see how people are attracted to each other based on gender. I am attracted to a person based on whether or not they understand me, if we have enough in common to enjoy each other's company and if they are a nice person. I guess you could say that I am less superficial about relationships than most because I do not base them on how people look or discriminate based on gender.

Case Study: Brad

I don't need to be physical. I am bothered by most touch. My wife is OK with this with one exception. She wanted to have a baby. I agreed that we would get pregnant and she is going to have a baby in three months.

Getting Along Well with Adults

We may know what to say and how to behave around people who are older, but have no idea how to interact or what to do with our peers. This can mask autism in some situations as parents and teachers do not readily notice signs of any difficulty. In these circumstances we are often described as "mature" and "responsible".

Case Study: Jimmy's Story

Jimmy came to the clinic when he was 13 years old. He was polite and charming. We had a delightful conversation about airplanes and he asked me about my family. Did I have children? How old were they? By the end of the day the team was on the fence about whether or not he had enough autistic characteristics to access services. We wanted more information to make our decision. So I sent our new evaluator fresh out of college to see how Jimmy interacted at school with other children his age.

The evaluator returned from her visit with the following report. "He seemed perfectly polite and normal to me. He paid attention and participated in class and was really well behaved."

"What did he do during lunch?" I asked.

"He ate his lunch and worked on his homework the entire time." She said.

"Did the other kids work on homework during lunch?" It was a rhetorical question. I was fairly certain that the other 7th grade boys were having burping contests, telling jokes and teasing girls.

As I gathered more information from the evaluator it became clear that while Jimmy interacted very well with adults, he didn't interact with children his age at all unless they approached him first. He would then politely respond to their question or requests and then go back to his homework.

His teacher reported that he was an "average" student, capable of getting "C's" in all of his classes but he often flunked tests. While he was liked by the other students he did not initiate any inter-actions with them and seemed uncomfortable in these situations. On the other hand, he regularly came to her when he needed help or to strike up a conversation about something that interested him.

While that in and of itself isn't enough to make anyone autistic, Jimmy had enough other characteristics that the team finally decided that he did meet the criteria for autism. Jimmy clearly had the ability to interact effectively with adults and they were often impressed by his mature behavior and conversation skills. But he was not comfortable relating to his peers and lacked the ability to do so.

Transitioning to Adulthood

Moving into adulthood can create a new set of problems for families. This is especially true for those of us who interacted with hugs, kisses and other forms of affection as children. The natural process is to shift from a relationship based on physical contact to one based on language and shared interests. But we often do not have the necessary language and social skills to interact in an adult manner. This can strain relationships as we shift from having interactions based on physical contact to a relationship where we have no idea how to relate. It can feel like a huge loss for siblings, family members and caregivers as we often isolate ourselves or engage in "parallel" activities where we may be in the same room but do not verbally interact with people.

Case Study: Matt

My wife had a very hard time with the changes our son was going through. He used to be very affectionate and we are a close family but when he turned 13 he became distant. He would not give hugs, would snap if we asked him a question and basically spent all his time in his room on the computer.

We got a late diagnosis and when we found out about the autism he got training and therapy to learn how to interact socially. It took a long time, about 3 years, but we stuck with it and eventually we were able to have a new relationship with him because he learned to talk to us and interact.

Addictions

Autistic people are at increased risk of addiction as a way to cope with the emotional and physical discomforts of life including the feeling of isolation, depression, sensory overload, and anxiety.

Case Study: Jeff

I have made the decision to quit drinking. I don't like the way it has become a part of my routine every night. At first it was one or two beers when the kids went down to unwind and now it's 3 or 4 after dinner with wine. I would like to find better ways to unwind that don't involve alcohol.

It's not unusual for people on the spectrum to be especially attracted to opiates because of their pain killing properties. Opiates include illegal substances like heroin and opium as well as prescribed medications like morphine, oxycodone and codeine.

Case Study: Ben

When I was younger I got involved with some of the wrong people and they introduced me to heroin. I have been clean for 3 years and still attend meetings to keep me straight. I didn't know what I was getting into at the time. I was just lonely and did what the guys around me did. I tried other drugs but none of the other ones did anything for me.

It is possible to become addicted to eating, exercise, television, pornography, sex, computer use, work or any other activity which serves the role of easing physical and/or emotional pain but also has negative consequences on relationships and life in general. Nadine discusses how the revolving door to addictions has impacted her life.

Case Study: Nadine

The doctor prescribed OxyContin after my surgery and it has been a problem ever since but what I realized when I finally decided to deal with my addiction is that I have been addicted to one thing or another for as long as I can remember. I was very regimented with my exercise routing even when I was a teenager and when I curbed my workouts I transferred that obsession to the computer. I have used these as an escape in my life even though I didn't realize it at the time, and I am just now learning to sit with my feelings instead of trying to numb them. I go to a cognitive behavioral therapist and attend a women's 12 step group which has helped.

Addictions and autism have a few things in common. Developmental delays, obsessive compulsive behaviors and social challenges are characteristics of both people on the spectrum and those who use a substance or activity to self medicate.

Case Study: David

David started smoking when he was 17. He had always struggled with keeping a conversation going if it wasn't about one of his interests but I could see how this became an even greater challenge for him with cigarettes. He withdrew even more as he anticipated his next opportunity to smoke. When he turned 19 he decided to quit and we saw all of his old behaviors that were there when he was a child, he did a lot more rocking and pacing, he wouldn't maintain conversations at all and he would get irritable about small things like looking for an outlet in a new place or a change in the schedule. Once David quit smoking we saw a lot more of his personality. He laughed more, and was able to have conversations again. Instead of just sitting in the room with people he would actually engage with us.

For people who are addicted and wanting to seek an autism evaluation it can be very difficult to see where the autism ends and the addiction begins. Early childhood information about behaviors is always important for an official diagnosis of autism, but it becomes even more important when identifying autistic individuals who use substances to self medicate.

> Addictions can magnify developmental delays, obsessive compulsive tendencies and social challenges in autistic people.

Those of us with addictions typically require very specialized supports to overcome these challenges as traditional treatments don't usually make sense for us or address our unique needs. Addiction programs should be equipped to handle the sensory, communication and socialization challenges unique to autism.

The Process of Healthy Bonding

Because people on the spectrum are faced with so many obstacles to feeling safe, the process of bonding and developing healthy attachments can take a significant investment in time and energy. This insecurity is the result of physical pain from hypersensitivity, seizures, gastro-intestinal issues or other medical complications coupled with the fact that our social communication skills may be delayed or at minimum distinctly different than yours.

Caregiver Guilt

Many parents and caregivers experience profound feelings of guilt when they learn that someone they love is autistic. When this discovery happens later on in life, that initial guilt is often magnified for not finding out earlier.

Case Study: Ben's Mom Marjorie

Ben always struggled through school but when he was in 5th grade teachers started reporting that he was willfully defiant and could do the work but just refused. I could tell they thought his problems were because I had done something to spoil my child.

Two years later he was diagnosed with autism and seizures. He wasn't being rebellious. He truly couldn't do the work because he was having so many seizures. But then I felt guilty about not catching it earlier so he could get the help he needed when he was little. I often wondered if it was something I had done to cause it.

This guilt doesn't help us and in some cases when we are very sensitive, it can actually hinder our connection with you as we pick up on and feel anxious about your feelings. What we really need from you is the opportunity to get in touch with our true nature, learn how to make decisions based on what is right for us and have acceptance from you.

Intuition, Authenticity & Connection

Intuition is the ability to be in touch with who you really are. *Authenticity* is listening to that inner knowing and making decisions based on this awareness of who you are. *Connection* is when two people interact authentically, honestly sharing aspects of themselves with each other to find common ground and trusting that each other's boundaries and differences will be mutually respected. In other words,

- ✓ If I am to truly know myself I must listen to my own intuition or inner voice
- ✓ If I am to live authentically I must follow this intuition instead of ignoring it
- ✓ If you and I are to have a connection I must share this honesty in exchange for your honest sharing in return

Accept then Expect

Often a parent or caregiver thinks- "First I will get my child to communicate and behave "normally". Then I will be able to connect with them." And while there is a lot of pressure on caregivers from society for parents to get their children to behave "normally" this approach is backwards. Just as we need to address our sensory and anxiety issues before we work on communication and social skills, we need to forge an authentic connection with you before we begin to learn how to socialize according to the expected norms of society.

Allowing us to recognize and follow our own intuition and then allowing for the honest exchange of connection comes first. Adaptation to social rules come naturally as a result of healthy connection.

Myth
If I teach my child communication and social skills first, they will then be better able to connect with me.

Fact
Create a healthy connection and social skills will naturally follow.

Case Study: Devon

Devon's parents called me when he was 13. They were concerned because he wasn't making any progress in speech therapy and I suspect in large part because he had recently broken most everything springy the house from jumping on it. The first thing I did when I met Devon was to take him outside to the backyard to jump on the trampoline. His father later told me that he thought I was crazy. After all, they had called me in because he was already jumping too much and they wanted me to help put a stop to the behavior, not encourage it.

Devon and I jumped for five or ten minutes in silence. Then I began to sing "My name is Devon". Devon repeated his name to the simple melody several times. Then I changed the words to "my favorite book is The Martian Chronicles by Ray Bradbury". His parents had told me that although he wasn't making progress in speech and hardly ever spoke he spent a significant amount of time reading books by Bradbury his favorite sci-fi author. So I knew the language was there inside his head. We just needed to find a way to bring it out. Devon repeated the phrase. After fifteen more minutes Devon and I were worn out and his parents said he talked more in that short time than he had all year long.

Instead of trying to get into a power struggle with Devon over jumping on the couch, I recommended that Devon's speech therapist incorporate the trampoline and music into her sessions and that his parents schedule regular times to jump on the trampoline together throughout his day.

Devon was communicating to us with his behavior every time he jumped on a couch or a bed that his body needed something and he was seeking it out in the best way he knew how.

By jumping with him on the trampoline people were communicating back to him that they understood he needed this experience.

Devon began to make rapid progress in speech therapy and no longer found the need to jump on things in the house. Four years later, Devon is still usually quiet but he does answer questions when asked and sometimes even offers information on his own when he is in a talkative mood.

Choose Your Battles

Ask yourself "what is the worst thing that could happen if:

_____?"

(insert behavior here)

When the consequences of that behavior are minor (no one will be injured, fired or incarcerated), then don't worry about it or feel the need to change it. Accept it instead as a personality trait that makes us unique.

- ✓ Sensory Behaviors (e.g. hand-flapping, spinning in circles, rocking back and forth, finger posturing, looking out of the side of eyes, looking at hands from the side of eyes, making guttural sounds, toe walking)

- ✓ Tick movements (e.g. head nodding, blinking eyes, twitches)

- ✓ Formal and repetitive language

- ✓ Needing to find and carry around the "right object" (e.g. rock, battery, pen, rubber band)

- ✓ Not allowing foods to touch each other on the plate

- ✓ Avoiding parties or social gatherings

- ✓ Having only one or two friends instead of many

- ✓ Interest in unusual subjects or obsessions

In these situations allow us to pay attention to our own instinct about what is true for us at that time instead of what is "right or wrong" according to society.

Follow Our Lead

Pay attention to our special interests and the coping skills we have already put in place for ourselves. You can help us maximize these tools instead of trying to eliminate them just as Devon was allowed to refocus his couch jumping energy towards jumping on the trampoline.

Our natural coping skills may include:

- ✓ Talking to imaginary friends
- ✓ Self-talk
- ✓ Visualizing a scenario or outcome before it happens
- ✓ Acting or taking on a "role", "character" or "persona"
- ✓ Dressing up or wearing costumes
- ✓ Sensory behaviors
- ✓ Taking breaks or leaving stressful environments
- ✓ Limiting new or stressful activities
- ✓ Playing video games or interacting on-line with others
- ✓ Watching movies
- ✓ Listening to music
- ✓ Reading
- ✓ Drawing
- ✓ Rhythmic activities like playing the drum or tapping furniture
- ✓ Interacting with animals

> *Pets can often act as a bridge to address specific challenges like the desire for physical contact in those of us who find touch painful. Therapy animals can also be trained to address a variety of issues including anxiety and reminders to wake up, take medication and eat or drink. Pets can help create the environment necessary for learning to take place for those of us who enjoy their company.*

Case Study: Jim

Jim has lived in the group home now for a couple years. He had trouble getting up in the mornings for his job and we tried everything from setting three alarms to using an amplifier to increase the volume. Then we got the therapy dog. She is trained to wake him up every morning and she just doesn't stop nudging him until he gets out of bed. Jim seems happier and better able to relate to us now that he has a companion.

Once you are aware of our instinctual coping tools you can help us to build on these in several ways:

1. Participate with us when these activities can include others (e.g. if we like to dress up and role play or make lists role play or make lists with us).

2. Provide us with necessary tools, space and supplies to further explore (e.g. if we like to smear our food or feces, give us alternatives like finger paints, shaving cream, peanut butter and pudding to smear in the tub or outside as an alternative).

3. Ask us questions about how our coping tools are useful for us.

4. Give us space to be alone if we need alone time as part of our coping.

The key to following our lead is to be in the moment. This is easier said than done when cell phones, televisions and round the clock responsibilities permeate every aspect of modern living. So put down the cell phone, turn off the television and be completely present. Focus on the interaction you are having with us.

Exercise #12: Follow Our Lead

Set aside 15-30 minutes with someone you care about who is autistic and participate fully in one of their favorite activities. The goal is to be completely in the moment and focus exclusively on them and their chosen activity.

The idea is for you to follow their lead and create a positive association in their mind between you and one of their favorite activities.

Here are the rules:

Activities can consist of but are not limited to role playing, watching leaves or sand fall, going for a walk, talking about an obsession, taking things apart, sensory activities building legos, watching a video, playing a game, listening to or singing songs, drawing, beating on a drum or playing another instrument.

Do you care about one of those people who has very limited interests? This exercise is for you too. If the only thing they like to do is watch the hamster run around the wheel, then watch the hamster together.

Phones, buzzers and televisions should be turned off so they do not become distractions.

Give and receive any physical contact during this time that is enjoyable to both of you (but do not feel obligated to do this step if physical contact is aversive).

Pay close attention to mannerisms, expressions & actions. Mirror them. (It's OK if they don't look directly at you. They may be picking up on more than you realize).

Case Study: Irene

Irene just turned 16. She has really grown up the past few years and recently started to ask me about my day and engage in some conversations. BUT, when she was 13 or 14 I was very worried because she didn't show any interest in other people. She could talk till the cows came home about what she wanted to on her terms but she would flat out ignore any comments or questions from any one who tried to engage with her. At that time she did a lot of parallel play with the neighbors and her cousins. Her therapist said to give her some time, that developmentally she was at that stage in her life.

I have to admit that it felt very one sided and uncomfortable to spend time around her but then I realized that my expectation for her to have a conversation with me was just not realistic for her developmental stage and so I learned to just enjoy doing activities in the same room together. It was a game changer for us. I realized that it was my unreasonable expectation not her behavior that prevented me from enjoying our time together because she just wasn't ready for the next step of interaction.

Coping with Emotions

Feelings are neither good or bad. They are a natural state of being based on how we interpret experiences, circumstances and relationships. Because of our unique challenges autistic people experience frequent feelings of frustration, fear and anger.

> **Myth**
> Anger, fear and sadness are negative emotions and they should be replaced with better emotions like happiness, love and serenity.

> ### Fact
> All emotions are a part of the body's internal guidance system or intuition. We need permission to listen to these emotions and be allowed to make authentic decisions based on these feelings.

This might sound counterintuitive but the goal in coping effectively with emotions is not to get rid of "negative" feelings only to replace them with "positive" ones. The goal is to help us identify and cope effectively with these messages by addressing whatever has triggered them.

When a person's feelings are minimized or dismissed by being told "cheer up", "it's not that bad" or "you should just be happy" this teaches us to ignore how we are really feeling and question our intuition. It also sends us the message that we are "OK" when we are happy and everything is going well but since you don't want to be around us when we are angry or afraid we are "not OK" when we experience these inevitable emotions. Instead of dismissing our feelings help us create an environment where we can:

- ✔ identify our feelings (whatever they are)
- ✔ understand them
- ✔ work through them in a constructive manner

This process teaches us to listen to our feelings and utilize them effectively to address circumstances, challenges and problems as they arise Sometimes just being able to say how we feel is helpful enough. Even if we don't know how we feel it is beneficial to hear about and start identifying specific feelings.

Exercise #13: Embrace Your Emotions

Here is a process that you can follow to help us cope effectively with our emotions.

Ask the following questions:

1. "You seem _____(insert emotion: scared, angry, frustrated). Is that right?" Sometimes we know how we feel and can confirm or deny your guess but if we don't know how we feel, move onto the next question anyway.
2. "What just happened?" or "What led up to you feeling _____?" If we don't know how we feel, you can share how you would feel in a similar situation at this point.
3. Acknowledge that the feeling(s) are normal given the circumstances.
4. "What can you do to _____(solve the problem or handle the situation)? Help us consider possible options to address the underlying event than prompted us to feel the way we do.

Being Authentic

We may listen to our inner voice and make decisions based on this instinct in some aspects of life yet be unable to make authentic decisions in other areas of life. Oftentimes for example we may be capable of being authentic in our career (especially when we can focus on our obsessions) but have a difficult time doing so in personal relationships.

Case Study: Brad

Because my job is based on my obsession with butterflies I am able to be fairly assertive and true to my nature at work. I don't have trouble speaking my mind even when other people may disagree or not see eye to eye. Not so in my personal relationships. I find that I am unable to state my preferences and make decisions when it comes to dealing with my family or on the rare occasion when I date. Even the most harmless of decisions like what to eat or which movie to watch are decisions I seem incapable of making. I will simply defer to others in these circumstances. I have been told that my sense of limited choice is also reflected in the options I give other people. I will inevitably say "do you want to do this or that" instead of the open-ended alternative. I am told most people suggest "what do you want to do?"

Part 1: Do you often agree to do things you don't want to do for some people?(put a check next to each one that applies to you)

_____ your boss

_____ your colleagues

_____ your siblings

_____ extended family

_____ clients

_____ acquaintances

_____ neighbors

_____ people at church and/or leisure activities

_____ people I do not know

_____ people I interact with on-line

_____ other: list_____

_____ Do you often agree to do things you do not enjoy because they are part of a routine, process or because other people are doing them?

_____ Do you often go places or behave a certain way to fit in or to avoid drawing attention to yourself even though it feels unnatural to you (e.g. stop sensory behaviors like rocking, or finger flicking or use informal language and gestures like "high five")?

Count each of the checks in part 1. The higher your score, the greater likelihood you struggle with being authentic in your life and the more likely you are to let people cross your boundaries.

Score: _____/13

Part 2: Do you know what your preferences and likes are in the following areas of your life? Put a check on each line if the answer is "yes".

Work/school activities

_____ tasks

_____ amount of time dedicated to tasks

Work / school space

_____ comfort

_____ appearance

Special interests and leisure time

_____ activities

_____ people

_____ amount of time dedicated

Marriage or dating relationships

_____ activities

_____ the kind of person you are attracted to

Family time

_____ activities

_____ people

_____ amount of time dedicated to family

Friends

_____ activities

_____ types of people you like

_____ amount of time dedicated

Holidays

　　　　_____ customs and traditions

　　　　_____ amount of time dedicated

Communication

　　　　_____ types (e.g. face-to-face, small group, large group, phone, e-mail, letter, chat, text)

　　　　_____ with who

　　　　_____ time limits

　　　　_____ in what circumstances and for what reasons

Food and dining

　　　　_____types

　　　　_____where food is eaten

　　　　_____who is with you

Clothing

　　　　_____comfort

　　　　_____appearance

New experiences and changes in plans

　　　　_____type

　　　　_____frequency

Part 3: Return to part 2 and ask yourself about dislikes for each of the listed categories. Put an X on the line next to those items where you or the person in mind have a good awareness of personal dislikes.

Score for Part 2 and 3: (count each of the items checked and X'ed above. The higher the score in part 2 and 3, the greater likelihood you or the person you are referring to are able to make choices that are in line with personal preferences and needs.

Score _____ /56

For those of you who like the abstract, answer the following questions:

What are your beliefs?

What are your core values?

What is your purpose in life?

Teaching the Social Rules

Once our sensory and anxiety needs have been met and you have created a healthy connection by meeting us where we are, we can then be receptive to learning social expectations. Social Rules define:

1. How people are supposed to behave

2. What to expect from other people

3. How to interact with each other

Teaching these norms is an important part of forging a connection because social rules allow us to know what the boundaries and expectations for behavior are. In other words when taught correctly and in the right order, they create a safe structure that allows us to know what we can and can't do. It may take us longer, require more practice and we may need skills to be broken down into small steps in order to understand some or all of the social rules.

Remember that learning social skills can be especially difficult for people on the spectrum because:

- ✓ We tend to focus on specialized details and may have a hard time seeing the big picture.

- ✓ We may have difficulty utilizing information or skills learned in one environment in other environments or with different people (this is known as the ability to generalize knowledge and skills).

- ✓ We may not see certain distinctions that are important to other people such as gender or social status.

- ✓ We may have language delays or processing difficulty.

- ✓ We may have difficulty with executive functioning or the ability to organize information and regulate our behavior.

- ✓ We may have interests that are not typical of others our age in intensity or subject matter.

✔ Social skills require abstract thinking and we tend to be very concrete and literal.

✔ We may strictly follow rules and expect others to do the same or get very anxious when these rules are not followed.

Not only is it common for us to learn abstract concepts later that our peers, but some skills and etiquette such as driving, parenting, work, dating and handling business by phone or email are specific to adult circumstances. This means we aren't exposed to the opportunity to learn some skills until we reach adulthood.

Myth
Adults have already learned the social skills they need to make it in life.

Fact
Adults need ongoing knowledge and training in social skills.

Case Study: Diana

The first time I went to visit Diana at college, she offered to caravan to the restaurant when she got off work. She didn't realize that she needed to keep an eye out and pace her driving so we could follow behind. She sped off and lost us before we even got out of the parking lot.

Some of the common areas we *may* need help with are:

- ✔ Greetings (shaking hands, saying 'hi' and 'goodbye', waving)
- ✔ Waiting in line
- ✔ Talking on the phone and making calls
- ✔ Talking in small groups
- ✔ Dressing appropriately (cleanliness, weather, neatness, occasion)
- ✔ Starting a conversation
- ✔ Body language (reading gestures and facial expressions, personal space)
- ✔ Figurative language
- ✔ Diplomacy and tact (stating opinions, deciding what to discuss with who, timing of conversations)
- ✔ Humor
- ✔ Identifying and dealing with emotions of self and others

Social skills are not always self evident and we might not understand how to apply these rules and interpret them. Even in situations where we are good about practicing a particular social rule, we may just be going through the motions and not understand the reason behind the rule.

It is therefore a good idea to let us know *why* we are learning a particular technique or skill. For example, if you teach the skill "asking questions about someone else's interests" let us know that asking questions about someone else's interests is one way to show that person you care about them and helps conversations be balanced. This understanding helps with the ability to generalize skills in different circumstances with a variety of people.

Putting it All Into Perspective

Developing a healthy connection begins by recognizing that we are not immune to the human experience. We often learn to "fake it" through our natural imitative abilities or receive training so that we can meet societal expectations. Just because we go through the motions does not mean we always understand why we are expected to follow these rules. This can make it difficult for us to figure out who we are and unless we truly know ourselves we will have a hard time connecting with others.

There are several circumstances that have an effect on our relationships with others and the better you understand these, the easier it is for you to support us. These special considerations include:

- ✓ Dealing with prejudice
- ✓ On-line communities and games
- ✓ Paranoia
- ✓ Mind reading
- ✓ Risk of burnout
- ✓ Perceptions of death and loss
- ✓ Crying
- ✓ Autistic parenting
- ✓ Sexual identity
- ✓ Getting along with peers
- ✓ Addiction

Healthy bonding takes time and effort. It relies on intuition, authenticity and positive shared interactions. Although the tendency is to try and teach social rules first in the hopes that positive relationships with follow, this is backwards. Create a trusting connection and social understanding will follow as a result of positive relationships.

Emotions are part of our internal guidance system. Instead of suppressing or ignoring them we should be supported in learning how to identify our feelings and recognize the role they play in communicating our needs.

Nathan was sentenced to 3 years and told his grandmother that he didn't want her to keep in contact with him. I suspected that Nathan actually refused contact to protect her from constantly worrying about him. I thought often about how his life could have been different if he had received supports when he was younger, or if the prosecution had been willing to consider rehabilitation over punishment. When Nathan was finally released he agreed to move into a supportive living environment with a roommate and reestablished contact with his grandmother. I visited him once he got settled in and he told me "That first time we met back in jail, I was pissed at you for bringing up Asperger's. I didn't want to accept my diagnosis. I was scared that having Asperger's would strip away my identity. But I had a lot of time to think while I was away and I couldn't drink or use drugs so I got clean. I'm not saying it was fun but it forced me to take a hard look at myself. The ironic thing is that when I finally came to terms with the Asperger's I was able to accept myself for who I am for the first time in my life. I plan to stay clean and I am looking for a job now."

I had worried that prison would hold Nathan back but he turned his experience into an opportunity to get to know and accept himself instead. I thought of the many people who walk around free from the physical chains he endured, but completely imprisoned inside their own minds instead. Being locked up gave Nathan the chance to break free from the idea that he had to pretend to be someone he was not. "I've learned to be my own best friend." he said and that is the perfect foundation for meaningful connection.

<u>To Do List</u>

_____Exercise #11: Social Expectations *(pg 136)*

     _____Part 1: Expectations

     _____Part 2: Adaptation

_____Exercise #12: Follow Our Lead *(pg 164)*

_____Exercise #13: Embrace Your Emotions *(pg 167)*

_____Exercise #14: Authenticity Screening Tool *(pg 169)*

*Why fit in when you were born to
stand out?*
Dr. Seuss

I want to just be allowed to BE.
Sue Taylor

The Next
Chapter
Write Your Own Story

---

*L*andon was institutionalized at age 16 for the regular and increasing habit of hitting people and throwing furniture. When I first met him he was being physically restrained two or three times a day and taking a concoction of medications that could probably kill a bison.

I was brought in to meet Landon because his team had tried everything they could think of to prevent these outbursts and they wanted to see if I could "fix the problem."

They took me to an office where I waded through a foot of unflattering records that had been building rapidly over the past several months in Landon's file.

Documentation from his behavior charts indicated that "aggressive behaviors" occurred more frequently just before scheduled class time and during the time his instructor was present and that in addition to autism he had a diagnosis of dysgraphia which meant he had a very difficult time writing and in his case tying his shoes.

I looked at his educational plan and right away I suspected what the problem might be. I asked to meet him and was escorted down a long hallway that smelled and looked like a hospital. Landon was pacing and staring out the window of his room. Above his bed was a shelf with books by Carl Sagan, Alan Lightman and Stephen Hawking.

"You like cosmology. I like cosmology too." I said and waited quietly.

Landon tensed, paced faster and then finally said "Yes. Yes I like cosmology. I like big bang, big bang theory, matter and energy, universal expansion."

He did not look at me but he grabbed Cosmos off the shelf and showed me a page, and then another and another, each time explaining the images in detail for me. I asked him questions and he excitedly answered. When it was time to say goodbye Landon made eye contact for a fleeting second then returned his gaze out the window.

Landon's team was waiting in the office to meet with me. "I think he's bored and frustrated with school." I told them. "He loves reading and learning about the universe but no one has ever explored this interest. Instead he is still being expected to learn to tie his shoes and write with a pencil even though he hasn't made any progress in either of these goals for 9 years".

We then talked in detail about how the instructor could focus Landon's curriculum around his natural interest in astronomy, physics and cosmology to keep him engaged in required subjects like math and English.

Two months later I got a call from his teacher. Landon's team had followed my recommendations and wanted to let me know how things were going. Landon was learning to type. He spent hours transcribing his cosmology books and he was no longer hitting or throwing furniture.

His teacher said "We really underestimated Landon's abilities. We just assumed that because he couldn't write he couldn't do other things either and we didn't give him the chance."

The solution is not always this readily apparent and improvements aren't always as drastic as they were for Landon but when positive change does happen it is because people are willing to make adjustments in their own perceptions and interactions. Awareness leads to understanding and understanding leads to effective solutions. The beauty of this reality is that you have the power to make a big difference in your relationship simply by redefining how you see someone.

Our journey together has been a process of addressing some of the most common misunderstandings about autism. If you have read this far, you already have the first key in hand and if you completed all the exercises then you are well on your way to having a good grasp of the other four keys which lead to healthy connection.

**Understanding
& Connection**

Key #5
Relate to Me

Key #1
Redefine Autism

Key #4
Learn My Language

Key #2
Turn "Problems"
Into Strengths

Key #3
Understand How
Sensory Integration
& Anxiety Affect
My Life

The goal of this book has been to help you create a shift in how you think but for those of you who like to apply what you learn in action-able ways, the following exercise is for you. Now that you have created a solid foundation, the next chapter is yours to write.

Exercise #15 Synthesis:

To help you synthesize the concepts in this book and the work you have already done, fill in the following blanks.

Synthesis

✔ **Key #1: Reframe Autism**

I have an understanding of the specific characteristics that are unique

to _____*(insert name)*.

List 5 of those characteristics below (e.g. splinter skills, humor, eye contact, tolerance for touch):

1._____

2._____

3._____

4._____

5._____

✔ **Key #2 Turn "Problems" into Strengths**

I am now able to see behaviors and qualities that once bothered me as possible strengths to be harnessed.

List 3 of these strengths below:

1. _____

2. _____

3. _____

✔ **Key #3: I understand how sensory integration and anxiety can have a profound effect on life**

List 3 ways sensory integration has an impact:

1. _____

2. _____

3. _____

List 3 ways anxiety currently affects life:

1._____

2._____

3._____

✔ **Key #4 Learn My Language**
List 5 communication techniques we use together:

1. _____

2. _____

3. _____

4. _____

5. _____

✓ **Key #5 Relate to Me**
List 3 special considerations that affect this person:

1._____

2._____

3._____

List 3 steps I have taken to help create a connection:

✓
1._____

2._____

3._____

<u>To Do List</u>

_____Exercise #15: Synthesis *(pg 182)*

Want more? Toni and her daughter Diana are available for
speaking, training, consultation and mentoring.

Connect with us at:
toni@toniboucher.net
512-986-0519

Made in the USA
Middletown, DE
20 October 2016